T0189518

Lecture Notes
in Business Information Processing

510

LNBIP reports state-of-the-art results in areas related to business information systems and industrial application software development – timely, at a high level, and in both printed and electronic form.

The type of material published includes

- Proceedings (published in time for the respective event)
- Postproceedings (consisting of thoroughly revised and/or extended final papers)
- Other edited monographs (such as, for example, project reports or invited volumes)
- Tutorials (coherently integrated collections of lectures given at advanced courses, seminars, schools, etc.)
- Award-winning or exceptional theses

LNBIP is abstracted/indexed in DBLP, EI and Scopus. LNBIP volumes are also submitted for the inclusion in ISI Proceedings.

Monika Malinova Mandelburger ·
Sérgio Guerreiro · Cristine Griffo · David Aveiro ·
Henderik A. Proper · Marianne Schnellmann
Editors

Advances in Enterprise Engineering XVII

13th Enterprise Design and Engineering Working Conference, EDEWC 2023
Vienna, Austria, November 28–29, 2023
Revised Selected Papers

 Springer

Editors
Monika Malinova Mandelburger
TU Wien
Vienna, Austria

Cristine Griffo
Free University of Bozen-Bolzano
Bozen-Bolzano, Italy

Henderik A. Proper
TU Wien
Vienna, Austria

Sérgio Guerreiro
University of Lisbon
Lisbon, Portugal

David Aveiro
University of Madeira
Funchal, Portugal

Marianne Schnellmann
TU Wien
Vienna, Austria

ISSN 1865-1348   ISSN 1865-1356 (electronic)
Lecture Notes in Business Information Processing
ISBN 978-3-031-58934-8   ISBN 978-3-031-58935-5 (eBook)
https://doi.org/10.1007/978-3-031-58935-5

This Springer imprint is published by the registered company Springer Nature Switzerland AG
The registered company address is: Gewerbestrasse 11, 6330 Cham, Switzerland

Paper in this product is recyclable.

Preface

This book contains the peer-reviewed research papers of the 13th Enterprise Design and Engineering Working Conference (EDEWC 2023). EDEWC 2023 was co-located with the 16th IFIP WG 8.1 Working Conference on the Practice of Enterprise Modeling (PoEM) 2023, as part of the Business Informatics (BI) Week 2023. The BI Week 2023 was hosted by the Business Informatics Group of TU Wien, Austria between 28th of November and 1st of December 2023.

In 2023 EDEWC was renamed from EEWC (Enterprise Engineering Working Conference)[1] (former CIAO! Enterprise Engineering Network (CEEN)) to include the notion of enterprise design in the title, and as such to broaden the scope of the conference. Enterprise design and engineering aims to take an integrative and engineering-oriented perspective to enterprise development management. As such, it considers enterprises as purposefully designed systems where all relevant aspects should be designed in coherence. The new scope of EDEWC reflects the rapid increase in digitalization of enterprises in the last decade. This has resulted in a substantial change in the nature and structure of enterprises, which was the main focus of EDEWC 2023.

Since 2005, the Enterprise Design & Engineering Network (EDEN) has organized the CIAO! Workshop and, since 2008, its proceedings have been published as *Advances in Enterprise Engineering* in the Springer LNBIP series. From 2011 onwards, this workshop was replaced by the Enterprise Design and Engineering Working Conference (EDEWC). The authors were involved in lively discussions with the audience about their presented papers, which resulted in the further development of the accepted research papers presented in these proceedings.

This volume contains the proceedings of EDEWC 2023, which received 15 submissions. In pursuit of the spirit of being a working conference, it is now the norm of EDEWC to publish the proceedings after the event. As such, the accepted papers that were presented during the conference were made available to the conference participants prior to the conference. This form facilitated lively discussions of the papers, which resulted in constructive feedback for the authors. After the conference and the paper presentations, the authors were able to revise and extend their papers by taking into account the feedback they received during the conference and the feedback from the reviewers, as well as by considering any new research developments that might have taken place during or after the conference.

Each submission was reviewed by three members of the Program Committee (PC). The reviews were double-blind. This means that neither the reviewers nor the authors were able to identify each other. Each submission received at least 3 reviews. On the basis of the reviews, the PC chairs made the decision whether to accept a paper or not. A total of 7 papers were accepted for presentation during EDEWC 2023 and publication in these Springer post-proceedings. Out of the 7 papers, 4 papers were accepted as full research papers, and 3 were accepted as short research papers. There was a possibility to promote

---

[1] https://ede-network.org/.

a short paper to a full paper. The promotion was contingent upon the potential for a research paper to be improved based on the feedback received during the presentation of the paper at the conference and the reviewers' comments. After the conference, the authors of 2 short papers submitted an improved version of their initial paper along with a report outlining the changes they had undertaken. The PC chairs reviewed these two papers and decided to promote one short paper to a full paper. As a result, these proceedings include 5 full research papers with 18–20 pages, and 2 short papers with 12–15 pages.

EDEWC aims to address the challenges that modern and complex enterprises are facing in a rapidly changing world. The participants of EDEWC 2023 shared a belief that dealing with these challenges requires rigorous and scientific solutions, focusing on the design and engineering of enterprises. The goal of EDEWC is to stimulate interaction between the different stakeholders, scientists, and practitioners interested in making enterprise engineering a reality.

We thank all the participants, authors, and reviewers for their contributions to EDEWC 2023 and hope that you find these proceedings useful to your explorations of current enterprise engineering challenges.

March 2024   Monika Malinova Mandelburger
                                                              Cristine Griffo
                                                              Sérgio Guerreiro

Organization

Steering Committee

David Aveiro	University of Madeira, Portugal
Henderik A. Proper	TU Wien, Austria
Mark Mulder	TEEC2, The Netherlands

Program Committee Chairs

Monika Malinova Mandelburger	TU Wien, Austria
Cristine Griffo	Free University of Bozen-Bolzano, Italy
Sérgio Guerreiro	INESC-ID & Instituto Superior Técnico, Universidade de Lisboa, Portugal

Proceedings Chair

Marianne Schnellmann	TU Wien, Austria

Program Committee

Stephan Aier	University of St. Gallen, Switzerland
Maurício Almeida	Federal University of Minas Gerais, Brazil
Eduard Babkin	Higher School of Economics, Nizhny Novgorod, Russia
Maria Das Graças Da Silva Teixeira	Federal University of Espírito Santo, Brasil
Jaap Gordijn	Vrije Universiteit, The Netherlands
Giancarlo Guizzardi	University of Twente, The Netherlands
Christian Huemer	TU Wien, Austria
Junichi Iijima	Tokyo Institute of Technology, Japan
Monika Kaczmarek-Heß	University of Duisburg-Essen, Germany
Petr Kremen	Babylon Health, UK and Czech Technical University in Prague, Czech Republic
Florian Matthes	Technical University of Munich, Germany
Graham McLeod	inspired.org, South Africa

Miguel Mira da Silva	INESC and University of Lisbon, Portugal
Hans Mulder	University of Antwerp, Belgium
Julio Nardi	NEMO/IFES, Brazil
Martin Op't Land	Capgemini, The Netherlands and University of Antwerp, Belgium
Carlos Páscoa	Portuguese Air Force Academy, Portugal
Robert Pergl	Czech Technical University in Prague, Czech Republic
Geert Poels	University of Gent, Belgium
Tatyana Poletaeva	INSA/LITIS, France
Stefan Strecker	University of Hagen, Germany
Linda Terlouw	Delft University of Technology, The Netherlands
Jan Verelst	University of Antwerp, Belgium

Additional Reviewers

Sven Christ
Aleksandar Gavric
Tri Huynh
Franziska Tobisch
Philip Winkler

Contents

Challenges in Building a Digital Business Ecosystem in the Maritime Domain

Ben Hellmanzik[(✉)] and Kurt Sandkuhl

Rostock University, Rostock, Germany
{ben.hellmanzik,kurt.sandkuhl}@uni-rostock.de

Abstract. The Marispace-X project aims to create a digital ecosystem of providers and users of data from the oceans. For this purpose, different use cases (munitions detection, biological climate protection, the construction of offshore wind platforms and the testing of IoT sensors) are used as examples to model the benefits of the planned ecosystem. One of the main focuses of the project is to analyze and build emerging business models. Most research in this sector is focussed on singular business models, while industry specific business models are underrepresented. The problems in building such an ecosystem are not only technical, but also social in nature. Therefore, this work aims to illustrate how academia and industry can work together to address problems and develop possible solutions for Digital Business Ecosystems (DBE). This conjunction of problems, i.e., the view of an industry domain as a business model and the view of digital business ecosystems, motivate this research. This work shows how to start building an ecosystem or platform and how to sensitize relevant stakeholders to existing challenges in designing ecosystems. Furthermore, some solution approaches are presented to address sub-problems in business model design, especially in the area of value creation through data. Lessons learned and further open challenges can be found at the end of the paper. The contributions of this paper are: (1) an emerging digital business ecosystem with different roles, (2) a problem/goal model for science-communication with relevant stakeholders, (3) the application of an analysis tool for business models with a FAIR-Data Value Chain, (4) remaining challenges, especially in the areas of ecosystem governance and modelling.

Keywords: Data value chain · FAIR · business model · Digital Business Ecosystem · Governance · Model

1 Introduction

The term "business model" has been used more and more frequently in recent times. In the literature database Scopus more than 45.000 different publications are available with a focus on some aspect of business models. A lot of these papers are concerned with the discussion about what a business model actually is and how it can be defined. Since the term is used in various fields, as for example

M. Malinova Mandelburger et al. (Eds.): EDEWC 2023, LNBIP 510, pp. 1–17, 2024.
https://doi.org/10.1007/978-3-031-58935-5_1

in economics and business information systems, it is no surprise that different interpretations have been developing over time. A recent development is the use of business models in the context of digital business ecosystems (DBE). A DBE is, according to [29] a "[...] socio-technical network of individuals, organisations and technologies that collectively co-create value."

The dominant view in investigating business models, however, is the "Enterprise View", according to Bernd Wirtz [34, p. 78]. This is a predominantly internal view of a business model, where resources, activities and the positioning of an enterprise are the important factors. The focus of this paper, however, is on the industry level: environmental factors, such as the role of customers and suppliers, as well as strategic partnerships play a bigger role in that regard. The collective co-creation of value leads to higher coordination costs along a project. Based on these assumptions, options must be developed to support the managers of a digital ecosystem. This includes, for example, new possibilities for modelling and cooperation. A lot of research in the area of digital business ecosystem, or more specifically platforms, follows an ex-post analysis. This leads to a distortion in the scientific approach, where only successful cases are researched. Additionally, this can lead to a lack of understanding regarding platform or ecosystem design [25]. To address these issues, research in the emerging digital business ecosystem Marispace-X was conducted.

Section 2 presents the core ideas and contents of Marispace-X and also defines important concepts. Sections 3 to 6 illustrate, how to start building an ecosystem and how to sensitize relevant stakeholders to existing challenges in designing ecosystems: starting from goal modeling for the ecosystem (Sect. 3), the investigation of value creation steps (Sect. 4), the relevant roles in the ecosystems (Sect. 5) and the business models for the ecosystem and involved roles (Sect. 6) are presented. Section 7 summarizes the challenges experienced in the project and Sect. 8 gives an outlook on future work.

The intended contributions of this paper are: (1) an emerging digital business ecosystem with different roles, (2) a problem/goal model for science-communication with relevant stakeholders, (3) the application of an analysis tool for business models with a FAIR-Data Value Chain, (4) remaining challenges, especially in the areas of ecosystem governance and modelling.

2   Marispace-X

The Marispace-X Project [21] is part of the Gaia-X Initiative: Gaia-X is an initiative that develops a software framework for control and governance and also defines a standardized catalog of policies and rules that can be applied to any existing cloud/edge technology stack. The goal is to achieve transparency, controllability, portability and interoperability of data and services. The framework is intended to be deployed on any existing cloud platform that adheres to the Gaia-X standard [10].

Gaia-X enables and promotes the creation of data spaces through trusted platforms governed by common rules that allow users and providers to share and exchange data securely and without restrictions on an objective technological basis across multiple actors [10].

The Idea behind Marispace-X is pretty simple: The Blue Economy is a growing opportunity for Business Models, for example in the areas of power generation in offshore-windparks, research, aquacultures, logistics, or the mining of resources [7]. But at the same time, the amount of available data skyrockets, while diversity in sensors and sensor formats increases. Best Practices are poorly defined and the development of common protocols takes time [31]. In effect, all of the 5 V's in Big Data are affected by these factors: The Volume of Data is increasing, the Variety of Data expanding, but the Veracity of Data is not as good managed as it could be, while the need for faster Velocity grows [20]. Possible solutions for these problems would also lead to better value creation processes.

Considering these aspects, the Value Proposition of Marispace-X is clear:

- Increasing efficiency and reducing costs through data-driven processes
- Cross-industry bundling and data availability through shared use
- Scaling through cloud technologies across applications and sectors in the maritime sector
- Developing new digital business models (e.g. federated algorithms/AI).

Further side effects include the development of future-oriented high-tech workplaces, knowledge-transfer between industry and research and an accelerated growth and digitization of the European Blue Economy [21].

The remaining question is: How to implement these Value Propositions? One of the answers is: Via platforms and a Digital Business Ecosystem (DBE).

The project partners in Marispace-X consist of different actors: Some are start ups or SME's, some are research institutes, some are universities and one is a Cloud Provider. The most important actors in this case were the de-facto project leaders: Two startups with the goal of building a data management platform for the maritime domain. The background of the CEO's of these companies varied, but they had a extensive legal background or a background in environmental geography and management.

In addition to an analysis of literature in the field, the most important entry points for our research were meetings and workshops with above stakeholders. Our first ideas were the following: while the theory of platforms could be too challenging for entrepreneurs, questions regarding the value creation in the maritime domain are more in their area of interest, especially with regard to effects of the FAIR-principles.

Thus, one of the early steps in the project was to build an easy to understand model to inform the project leaders of risks or opportunities in platform ecosystems. The background for this decision can be found in De Reuver et al.'s work [25]. According to the authors, a clear definition of platforms and ecosystem is necessary. In addition to that, the scope of the work must be clear and concepts be defined.

In order to achieve that, it should be specified here, that we have a sociotechnical view on platforms. The unit of analysis is the business model of the ecosystem partners, starting from view of the platform owner. The underlying definition of a platform is that from Parker et al. [23]:

"*A platform is a business based on enabling value-creating interactions between external producers and consumers. The platform provides an open, participative infrastructure for these interactions and sets governance conditions for them. The platform's overarching purpose: to consummate matches among users and facilitate the exchange of goods, services, or social currency, thereby enabling value creation for all participants.*"

For the definition of a platform ecosystem we rely on Hein et al. [12]:

"*A digital platform ecosystem comprises a platform owner that implements governance mechanisms to facilitate valuecreating mechanisms on a digital platform between the platform owner and an ecosystem of autonomous complementors and consumers.*"

Since there are different types of platforms, it could be interesting to see which one Marispace-X aspires to be. For that discussion, the distinction between a transaction and an innovation platform, proposed by Cusumano, Gawer and Yoffie [11] could be of use.

3   Goal-Modelling and Stakeholder Participation

None of the participating stakeholders had experience in modelling or building ecosystems, so the most common goals and challenges in the Design of Platforms were modelled by a researcher. The provision of those more general and abstract model should lead to a more precise strategic alignment in the ecosystem.

The modelling language used was 4EM, the underlying model a Goal-Model according to Sandkuhl et al. [28]. It should be noted that the goals presented are not necessarily SMART. These goals are not **S**pecific enough, at these Stage hardly **M**easurable, but **A**chievable and **R**elevant. The timeboundness of the goals is rather broad. Also, the approach to modeling was not collaborative, but merely an individual approach. In this context, there is need for clarification: In this case the presentation of the model was more important than the modeling process: The most important findings from the research were to be presented to the industry partners in a form as possible, since companies in the startup phase in particular have relatively little time to spare.

Although the concept of a "prosumer" is sometimes of interest in platform research, since participants produce and consume at the same time [2], this concept is not applied in the modelling approach. This differentiation between consumers and producers on a platform could seem to be more distinct and better understandable by practitioners. One of the most prominent examples of platform building problems seems to be the "chicken-or-the-egg" problem [30]. The question is whether to attract users or to bring complementarians onto the platform first. Therefore, these are two of the views of the target problem model. One of the goals connected to that area is the "Capturing" of values, as proposed by Rohn et al. [26], with the different subgoals, seen in Fig. 1.

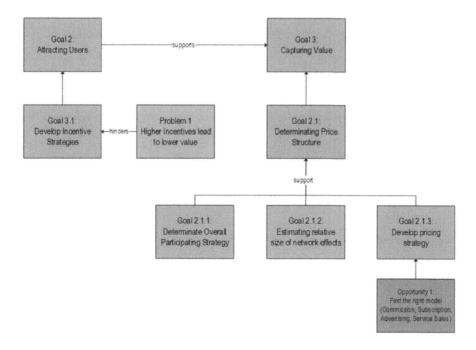

Fig. 1. User and Value Capturing Perspective in a Goal Model

The next area is that of Value Creation: How is value created on a platform? We still rely on the work of Rohn et al. [26] here, the results can be seen in Fig. 2.

But since the creation of value on a platform is mostly done by the complementors of the platform, not the platform owner [27] (p. 23), the complementor side is of special interest in platform development.

Here, the attraction of different organisations and stakeholders could be a great opportunity [15], but a risk at the same time. Here, observing the strategic dimension, proposed by Kretschmer et al. [19] could help to balance the cooperation and competition between participants. Brunswicker et al. [4] emphazise here to find a balance between platform openness and restrictive access. Hesenius et al. [16] promote the alignment of technical and business architecture, the focus on platform features and the reduction of technical prerequisites for service providers. Multihoming could be seen as a problem [27] (p. 101), while problems between ownership concerns are mostly in the area of personal data [27] (pp. 15, 135), the usage of data could be of interest for developers on a platform too. The results of the models can be seen in Figs. 3 and 4.

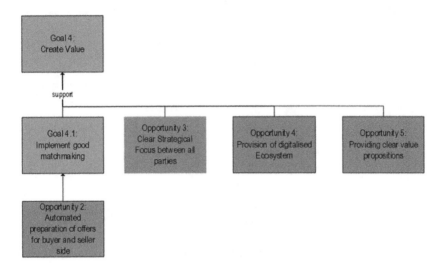

Fig. 2. Value Creation in a Goal Model

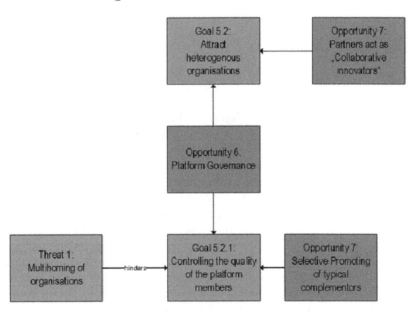

Fig. 3. Attraction of Complementors in a Goal-Model

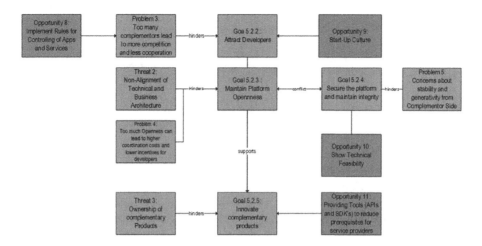

Fig. 4. Attraction of Developers in a Goal-Model

These models were the basis for conversation between the researchers and the CEO's, the CFO and the CMO of the participating leading SME's in Marispace. Together, a joint understanding was formed: Both of the enterprises were not a platform at the moment, they had a more strategic approach to data management in the maritime domain, not platform theory. But one of the findings of Sethi et al. [30] was still the basic idea behind their business idea: The focus on a niche market (in this case more geographically) to test the value proposition.

4   Shifting the View to Value Creation

From a research point of view, this meant a shift in the viewpoints of the challenges: Instead of platform governance issues, the challenges here were more or less business model challenges in nature. To understand these, the concept of the data value chain and some of the insights of interviews with stakeholders were applied. One of the CEO's made the need for standardised formats in the maritime domain very clear: More than 14 different software suites would be needed to analyse all of the different kinds of sensors.

One of the solutions to that problem would be the FAIR-Principles, Data should be Findable, Accessible, Interoperable and Reusable [33]. For the maritime domain there is one example of such a Value Chain by Ferreira et al. [9], however the step of "Value Curation" has not stated the FAIR-Principles explicitly. Additionally, some of the benefits of the Value Chain from a business point of view was not given.

The task for research here was to develop a Data Value Chain with the FAIR-Principles in mind, which was done by adding the steps Meta-Data Generation, Assessment and Qualification, Licencing and Sovereignity, as well as Indexing and Registering [14] (Fig. 5).

Fig. 5. FAIR-Data Value Chain

Then, an analysis tool was build to specify the Value Proposition of the respective Business Model. The idea behind the tool stems mostly from the Partial Models in a Business Model of Bernd Wirtz [34](p.126). This approach was used for three reasons: First, the Osterwalder Canvas [22] was already familiar in the participating company. The re-execution of the modelling experience was therefore not a promising approach. The use for an internal view of the canvas can be beneficial, but from our research point of view it was not sufficient enough. First of all, it did not take the challenges in the maritime domain itself into account. The value proposition canvas could be of help here, but the mere question of pains and gains would not show an understanding of the (industry-wide) data value chain. The third reason against the use of the Osterwalder Canvas was the reliance on the Data Value Chain from Edward Curry [6], who in turn uses the Value Chain from Michael Porter [24]. The Concept of the Value Chain as a "system of interdependent activities" as it is called by Porter is the basis of our understanding of the different linkages in a business model. This linkage between different activities is not so clear in the Osterwalder Canvas itself. One result of our research is therefore an Analysis tool, that links different parts of business models with network partners in an industry view. As for different modelling methods, like e3-Value: The project is momentarily in a design phase, not a deployment phase. Modelling of economic values as it is the focus of e3-Value [18] would therefore be highly theoretical, while the development for a joint understanding of an DBE must be found between different partners. The first step of the Modelling is therefore analysing the market and the different stakeholders in the domain and the ecosystem, not the modelling with specific values.

The analysis tool covers mostly the elements of strategy, networks and value creation. The idea is to get to a market offer model (or defining the value proposition) via this tool. One Axis represents the Data Value Chain, the other one represents questions regarding the partial models of business [13]. Since one of the goals in the platform business model has to be standardisation, "Architectures and Tools" were added as a means to define the market offering, as well as input and output data to "visualise" what happens to the data. The core question was always that of value creation (Fig. 6).

The combination of those two axes results in a Matrix, which is fillable by the participants and can be seen in Fig. 7.

This leads to a "guiding" Framework for an interview: For each step in the Data Value Chain the participants are asked basically the same questions: How

Fig. 6. Analysis Dimensions: Blue - Value Creation, Green - Network Model, Beige - Strategy (Color figure online)

Fig. 7. Analysis Matrix

would you describe the step for your company? Are there any tools or architectures for that? What is it you do to create value in that area? What is the input in this step? What is the output? What is the challenge here? Are there any new trends? Who is active in that area?

If the need arises, the clarification of some terms could be useful and the questions may lead to follow up questions.

In the resulting interview with Matrix Application, the feedback on the tool was good: One of the involved stakeholders pointed out the end of the data value chain and said "This is the part where we would do fancy presentations, for the application and maybe the Use of AI. But the start of the value chain is actually more important for us.". There may be some changes to do in the application of the matrix to reach a joint understanding: In this use-case for example, the proposed term "Data Acquisition" was substituted with the term "Data Upload". This joint understanding will be important later on, when more than one stakeholder joins the modelling. The joint understanding should therefore be considered from the perspective of a consortium, not a single individual on the producer or consumer side. However, the producer side seems to be a better starting point.

5 Identified Roles in the Ecosystem

These tasks seemed sufficient for the moment, the research direction went back to a more general approach: To realise an ecosystem, the definition of roles is an important one [32].

For the strategic alignment, the proposed roles from the project "incentives and economics of data sharing" (IEDS) were used: In a workshop, the relevant stakeholders in the project gathered and were presented with all of the options and their own view of the ecosystem. The self-identification process lead to the following roles in the ecosystem: Service Provider, Cloud Platform Provider, Data-Infrastructure Provider. The role of Data provider was left empty via-self identification, but the participants saw one absent participant in the role, who could not participate in the workshop. More interestingly, the role of the ecosystem orchestrator was left empty: The responsibility here was not clear. From a research standpoint, this could be because all of the participants gather in monthly meetings in a consortium and come to agreements there. This could be mapped when the concept of the ecosystem orchestrator represents the same as the platform owner in Hein's [12] depiction of a platform. Another possibility is that the responsibility here is still unclear, which in turn could lead to frictions.

Proceeding from these observations, a general business model for the platform was build via the framework of Wirtz [34]. The understanding of a business model here is as follows:

"A business model is a highly simplified and aggregated representation of the relevant activities of a company. It explains how the value-added component of a company generates marketable information, products and/or services. In addition to the architecture of the value creation, the strategic, as well as the customer and market components are taken into account to ensure the overall goal of generating or securing the competitive advantage." [34].

The modelling was structured according to the partial Models of Wirtz. While modelling the industry specific prototype, we understood the socio-technical system as one company, consisting of the core members of the project. The **strategy model** defines the strategic business areas of the company and the long-term and medium-term goals in the business areas, including the activities to achieve them. The **resource model** identifies core assets and competences, which are important for value creation. Core assets are company-specific, are difficult for competitors to develop or imitate and are of great importance for the value creation process. Similarly, core competences are company-specific, central to the value proposition and difficult for competitors to acquire or develop. The **network model** defines the most important strategic partners of the company. The **market offer model** structures the existing market and competitive situation, defines the company's focus and identifies potentially competing business models. The **customer model** defines which value propositions (i.e. products, services or combinations thereof) are offered to which combinations are offered to which customer groups in which market segments. This also includes differentiation criteria and utilisation scenarios for the products and/or services offered. The **revenue model** structures the cash flows and defines their significance. It shows how the value creation for the company can be monetised. The **value creation model** defines how the input factors (e.g. goods or services) are combined and transformed into value offerings (e.g. products and/or services) of the company. In the case of Marispace-X the Value Creation process can generally described via the mentioned data value chain, where the singular steps add value to the input data, up to the point of a new product or a new service. The **finance model** describes the sources of capital required for value creation and the associated supporting business activities. The **procurement model** defines which production factors are provided by which supplier. The resulting model can be seen in Fig. 8.

6 A Generic Business Model for Marispace-X

The funding from the project stems from mostly public institutes, who want new standards and more opportunities for business models in exchange. The Value Creation process in the platform is the FAIR-Data Value Chain, generally speaking for all involved parties. The market offer model is derived from the application of the FAIR-Data Value Matrix (in this case, the market offer is cost reduction through standardisation, interoperability (A "One fits all" approach, Network effects, and derived from interviews, the visualisation of data.) The revenue can be earned via value based pricing (according to Hinterhuber [17] a promising approach) or subscription models from different customers or better "complementors". The strategy dimension starts small in a niche market and transforms from a data management solution to a transaction platform and then (hopefully) to an innovation platform. The competencies in the maritime domain are strong and backed by research institutes and expertise. Infrastructure and Cloud Infrastructure are taken care of by senior developers. The network model is strong with different kinds of partners in various areas of the platform. The management of the partners follows the concept of "tier lists" and should lead to manageable governance decisions. The customers of the resulting business model could be fishers, offshore-wind farm operators, shipping and insurance companies (since the cost of insurance of natural habitat are quite expensive, as well as construction work underwater), or possibly sea-weed farmers in the future. This model does not include other forms of new business models or opportunities yet, but can be build on in a later iteration.

The remaining challenge here is to model the relationships of the stakeholders in an easy to understand way. In order to achieve this, the different business models of the stakeholders will be investigated and possible connections in a model revealed. But there were more challenges in different aspects of the ecosystem, which will be collected in the next section.

Alternatively, there are different business models for each of the participating members in the ecosystem. They were organised according to their role (e.g. Data Provider). An example of that approach can be seen in Fig. 9.

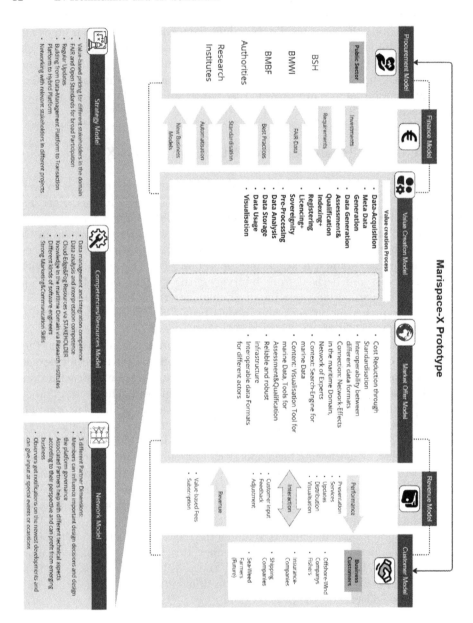

Fig. 8. A generic Business Model for Marispace-X

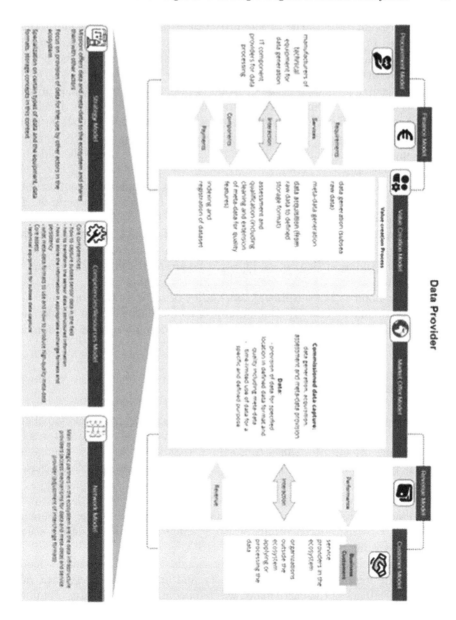

Fig. 9. A generic Business Model for the role "Data Provider"

7 Challenges During the Project

One of the more obvious challenges in the project is the organisation: With lots of different stakeholders, who need to interact on a regular basis, while employee fluctuation is high, the organisation is difficult.

Another point is the niche in the project: The different sensors and formats may have led to a specialisation in an already narrow space. The need for standardisation is high, but the gathering of the relevant experts in the field for standardisation may be very difficult.

One reoccurring concern is the question of pricing of data: What is my data worth? While the price for research in the maritime domain is high, the sharing of data is still a difficult venture. Some researchers like Enders et al. [8] argue, that lack of management support could bring data sharing prospects to a halt. How to involve management of external companies in these decisions could be a important question.

Another point is the "Chicken-or-Egg" problem disguised in another form. It regards the question of how a community can be build from scratch. The incentives here could be another interesting topic.

Deriving from these arguments, the research of value co-creation, which is an important part in platforms [35] has not been investigated thoroughly in the project. The studies of Benz et al. [3] could be an interesting starting point for that challenge.

The last point is not surprising, since a lot of software developments "fail" in regards to time or cost [1]. But in an ecosystem, delays in the development lead to a more severe impact, since all participants are interwoven. Finding and fixing these bottlenecks could be a crucial challenge.

8   Summary and Future Work

In this case-report, we worked on Modelling and Analysing Approaches in Digital Business Ecosystems in the maritime domain. Focus of the approaches was one of the leading organisations in a consortium, that wants to realise change and a digital transformation in the maritime domain. The key problems (lack of standardisation, high-costs, different actors) were analysed. The researchers role in the project is to develop business models for the partners in the ecosystem and the industry itself. The researchers themselves are part of the consortium, so that our research approach falls between action research and design science research according to Collatto et al. [5].

Our task at hand was the creation of a industry specific business model, incorporating findings from platform theory and approaches of the data value chain. The feedback of the participants was important, as it implicates usefullness to the project. The incorporation of platform theory and the goals defined by research were interesting starting points, but not feasible for the design phase of a digital business ecosystem, since most of the research conducted on platforms was ex-post [25]. The goals in the project therefore shifted to analysis and tools for anaylsis which were better suited to get an understanding of the maritime industry.

In order to achieve these tasks:

- A explorative literature review on platforms was conducted

- The main findings of the literature review were presented in a goal/problem model
- The results were presented to a stakeholder
- The feedback of the stakeholders was incorportated in research (important and interesting, but not in the right phase)
- A structured literature review lead to the connection of FAIR-Data with a Data Value Chain
- The FAIR-Data Value chain was connected with different parts of business models, as a means to develop an anaylsis tool
- The analysis tool (the FAIR-Data Matrix) was presented to the stakeholder
- The analysis tool was deemed appropriate for the task of analysing the data value chain of the maritime industry, and only slightly changed
- The tool was used in another interview with a research institute
- The results were used to develop a industry specific business model for the maritime domain, incorporating different viewpoints
- The industry specific business models lead to further open questions of Modelling a Digital Business Ecosystem, which were incorporated in a modelling workshop

In this work, a possible approach was shown to scientifically accompany the industrial work in building ecosystems. Since work is currently still being done on the project, a new perspective on the development of platforms is shown, which is not only ex-post. For this purpose, current problems of data processing in the maritime domain were worked on and scientifically highlighted. Solutions and analysis tools were presented to the industry partners to be able to look at these problems from a different perspective and to sharpen their own business model.

Future work should include participative modelling with relevant stakeholders for a holistic ecosystem view, the analysis of generic business models for the roles in the ecosystem and possibly work on governance models in the ecosystem.

References

1. Ahimbisibwe, A., Cavana, R., Daellenbach, U.: A contingency fit model of critical success factors for software development projects. J. Enterp. Inf. Manag. (Emerald), **28**(1), 7–33 (2015)
2. Alonso-López, N., Sidorenko-Bautista, P., Apablaza-Campos, A.: Tiktok and active audiences in processes for political and structural change. An exploratory study based on the Scottish referendum. Commun. Soc. **36**(3), 87–101 (2023)
3. Benz, C., Riefle, L., Schwarz, C.: Co-creating value in B2B platform ecosystems – towards a deeper understanding of the emergence and nature of actor engagement. In: Ahlemann, F., Schütte, R., Stieglitz, S. (eds.) WI 2021. LNISO, vol. 46, pp. 236–242. Springer, Cham (2021). https://doi.org/10.1007/978-3-030-86790-4_17
4. Brunswicker, S., Schecter, A.: Coherence or flexibility? The paradox of change for developers' digital innovation trajectory on open platforms. Res. Policy **48**(8) (2019)

5. Collatto, D., Dresch, A., Lacerda, D., Bentz, I.: Is action design research indeed necessary? Analysis and synergies between action research and design science research. Syst. Pract. Action Res. **31** (2018)
6. Curry, E.: The big data value chain: definitions, concepts, and theoretical approaches. In: Cavanillas, J.M., Curry, E., Wahlster, W. (eds.) New Horizons for a Data-Driven Economy, pp. 29–37. Springer, Cham (2016). https://doi.org/10.1007/978-3-319-21569-3_3
7. Dalton, G., et al.: Feasibility of investment in blue growth multiple-use of space and multi-use platform projects; results of a novel assessment approach and case studies. Renew. Sustain. Energy Rev. **107** (2019)
8. Enders, T., Satzger, G., Fassnacht, M.K., Wolff, C.: Why should i share? Exploring benefits of open data for private sector organizations. In: PACIS 2022 Proceedings: AI-IS-ASIA (Artificial Intelligence, Information Systems, in Pacific Asia). AIS eLibrary (AISeL) (2022)
9. Ferreira, J., et al.: Maritime data technology landscape and value chain exploiting oceans of data for maritime applications. In: 2017 International Conference on Engineering, Technology and Innovation (ICE/ITMC), pp. 1113–1122 (2017)
10. Gaia-X: What is gaia-x? (2023). https://gaia-x.eu/what-is-gaia-x/
11. Gawer, A.: Digital platforms' boundaries: the interplay of firm scope, platform sides, and digital interfaces. Long Range Plan. **54**(5), 102045 (2021)
12. Hein, A., Schreieck, M., Riasanow, T., Soto Setzke, D., Wiesche, M., Böhm, M., Krcmar, H.: Digital platform ecosystems. Electron. Mark. 1–12 (2019, in press)
13. Hellmanzik, B., Sandkuhl, K.: A data value matrix: linking fair data with business models. In: Nurcan, S., Opdahl, A.L., Mouratidis, H., Tsohou, A. (eds.) RCIS 2023. LNBIP, vol. 476, pp. 585–592. Springer, Cham (2023). https://doi.org/10.1007/978-3-031-33080-3_41
14. Hellmanzik, B., Sandkuhl, K.: Towards a fair-ready data value chain for dataspaces. In: Griffo, C., Guerreiro, S., Iacob, M.E. (eds.) EEWC 2022. LNBIP, vol. 473, pp. 90–105. Springer, Cham (2023). https://doi.org/10.1007/978-3-031-34175-5_6
15. Helmond, A., Nieborg, D.B., van der Vlist, F.N.: Facebook's evolution: development of a platform-as-infrastructure. Internet Hist. **3**(2), 123–146 (2019)
16. Hesenius, M., Usov, A., Rink, C., Schmidt, D., Gruhn, V.: A flexible platform architecture for the dynamic composition of third-party-services. In: Proceedings - 2019 IEEE International Conference on Software Architecture - Companion, ICSA-C 2019 (2019)
17. Hinterhuber, A.: Customer value-based pricing strategies: why companies resist. J. Bus. Strateg. **29** (2008)
18. Kostova, B., Gordijn, J., Regev, G., Wegmann, A.: Comparison of two value-modeling methods: e3 value and seam. In: 2019 13th International Conference on Research Challenges in Information Science (RCIS), pp. 1–12 (2019)
19. Kretschmer, T., Leiponen, A., Schilling, M., Vasudeva, G.: Platform ecosystems as meta-organizations: implications for platform strategies. Strateg. Manag. J. (2020)
20. Lytra, I., Vidal, M.E., Orlandi, F., Attard, J.: A big data architecture for managing oceans of data and maritime applications. In: 2017 International Conference on Engineering, Technology and Innovation (ICE/ITMC), pp. 1216–1226 (2017)
21. North.io: Marispace-x (2022). https://de.marispacex.com/
22. Osterwalder, A., Pigneur, Y.: Business Model Generation: A Handbook for Visionaries, Game Changers, and Challengers, vol. 1. Wiley, Hoboken (2010)
23. Parker, G., van Alstyne, M., Choudary, S.P.: Platform Revolution: How Networked Markets are Transforming the Economy - And How to Make Them Work for You, 1st edn. W.W. Norton & Company, New York and London (2016)

24. Porter, M.E.: Competitive Advantage: Creating and Sustaining Superior Performance. Free Press, New York and London (1985)
25. de Reuver, M., Sørensen, C., Basole, R.: The digital platform: a research agenda. J. Inf. Technol. **33** (2017)
26. Rohn, D., Bican, P.M., Brem, A., Kraus, S., Clauss, T.: Digital platform-based business models - an exploration of critical success factors. J. Eng. Technol. Manag. **60**, 101625 (2021)
27. Ronteau, S., Muzellec, L., Saxena, D., Trabucchi, D.: Digital Business Models: The New Value Creation and Capture Mechanisms of the 21st Century. De Gruyter, Berlin and Boston (2023)
28. Sandkuhl, K., Wißotzki, M., Stirna, J.: Vorgehensweise und Notation der 4EM-Methode. In: Sandkuhl, K., Wißotzki, M., Stirna, J. (eds.) Unternehmensmodellierung. Xpert.press, pp. 107–201. Springer, Heidelberg (2013). https://doi.org/10.1007/978-3-642-31093-5_8
29. Senyo, P.K., Liu, K., Effah, J.: Digital business ecosystem: literature review and a framework for future research. Int. J. Inf. Manag. **47**, 52–64 (2019)
30. Sethi, K., Biswas, B., Balodi, K.C.: Mobilizing B2B electronic marketplace: an exploratory study of critical success factors among Indian start-ups. Glob. Bus. Rev. 097215092110056 (2021)
31. Tanhua, T., et al.: Ocean fair data services. Front. Mar. Sci. **6**, 92 (2019)
32. Tsai, C.H., Zdravkovic, J., Stirna, J.: Modeling digital business ecosystems: a systematic literature review. Compl. Syst. Inform. Model. Q. **30**, 1–30 (2022)
33. Wilkinson, M.D., et al.: The fair guiding principles for scientific data management and stewardship. Sci. Data **3**, 160018 (2016)
34. Wirtz, B.W.: Business Model Management: Design - Instrumente - Erfolgsfaktoren von Geschäftsmodellen, 5. aufl. edn. Gabler, Wiesbaden (2010)
35. Zimmermann, A., Schmidt, R., Jugel, D., Möhring, M.: Evolution of enterprise architecture for intelligent digital systems. In: Dalpiaz, F., Zdravkovic, J., Loucopoulos, P. (eds.) RCIS 2020. LNBIP, vol. 385, pp. 145–153. Springer, Cham (2020). https://doi.org/10.1007/978-3-030-50316-1_9

Multi-agent Simulations of Mutual Trust Management Strategies as a Base of Innovative Organizational Forms Engineering

Eduard Babkin, Vitalii Golov, and Pavel Malyzhenkov[(✉)]

Department of Information Systems and Technologies, National Research University – Higher School of Economics, Bol. Pecherskaya 25, 603155 Nizhny Novgorod, Russia
{eababkin,pmalyzhenkov}@hse.ru

Abstract. The emergence of the new business context is creating innovative systems and models of work, having a deep impact on business environment and organizational interdependencies. In many modern cases such systems consist of a network of business agents which are autonomous in their behavior, believes and values, but should maintain interaction between each other in order to enhance overall innovation capacity and competitiveness. Distributed and cooperative multi-agent networks should be considered as an inimitable asset and collaborations and networks encompass a broad range of inter-organizational or even inter-personal relationships. These forms of conducting business activity are characterized by a low volume of transaction costs and the grade of mutual trust between the agents represents the crucial factor for its formation. This work applies the concept of multi-agent simulations to study impact of alternative trust management strategies on the overall effectiveness of the enterprise. A real case of the software freelance market is used for simulation experiments based on the NetLogo multi-agent platform. Analysis of simulations shows that cognitive trust management strategies give advantage even in environments with a high level of information noise. Developed multi-agent decentralized algorithms were generalized and can be applied for automation of routine tasks in other domains where trust management in networks of cooperative agents plays an important role.

Keywords: transaction costs · trust · Industry 4.0 · Industry 5.0 · organizational interaction · multi-agent simulation

1 Introduction

The emergence of the Industry 4.0 and the consequent transition to Industry 5.0 as a new social and business context is creating innovative systems and models of work, having a deep impact on business environment and organizational interdependencies [18]. The importance of this latter consists in the more attentive focus onto human-centric values where the trust plays the important role. To define the current business landscape, some authors [3, 6, 7] indicate that one of its basic feature is the intricate interdependency among companies that requires an alternative framework to be studied. The disruption that the fourth industrial revolution will have on existing political, economic and social models will therefore require that empowered actors recognize that they are part of a distributed power system that requires more collaborative forms of interaction to succeed [18].

Different sources [2, 3, 6] recognize business relationships as another type of resource that a company can use in the strategic game. The opportunity to mobilize others as "partners" has increasingly become an emergent issue in the management literature. From a resource-based perspective the importance of business relationship is emphasized by the idea that a firm's critical resources may span the boundaries of the firms. It is often claimed that a firm's network of business partners should be considered as an inimitable resource itself and as a means by which to assess others' inimitable resources. The multi-agent networks are to be considered inimitable because of their flexibility and the capacity to adopt to any business situation. So, in these studies collaborations and networks encompass a broad range of inter-organizational relationships.

Business networks can also be analyzed as a result of an engineered process [7], where the working arrangements are fulfilled in a formal organization, the goals are planned and specified in a predetermined time horizon, the cooperation is based on "network capital" rooted in a business and economic rationality and focused on investing in relationships as a means to increase business performances. The architectural approach helps to balance 'market-driven' perspective (focused on customer's needs) with a 'technology-driven' approach (focused on internal technology aspects).

Transaction cost economists [2, 3, 19] have argued that the cooperation may assume different forms between markets and hierarchy and these forms depend on the volume of transaction costs associated with a specific exchange on the market or inside the vertical integration [3]. In transaction cost economic literature various roles have been identified for collaboration issues, but the grade of the mutual trust between the agents remains the most important factor of transaction costs volume. Hence, the possibility to manage and define the trust gives the opportunity to define the success of different organizational forms and justify the necessity of business engineering processes application.

In this article we consider application of multi-agent simulations to study impact of alternative trust management strategies on the overall effectiveness of the enterprise. Within that scope we consider trust as a social phenomenon and apply socio-cognitive approach to its definition following Castelfranchi and Falcone [4]: trust is a certain state in terms of individual agent's beliefs and intentions which emerges during social interactions when the agent decides to rely on another agent(s), despite the possibility of harm or negative consequences.

We believe that objectivation and operationalization of trust management in the form of multi-agent simulations will open opportunities for design of efficient Industry 5.0 enterprises, where humans and artificial agents collaborate together and dynamically form business networks. A real case of the software freelance market is used for simulation experiments based on the NetLogo multi-agent platform. Analysis of simulations shows that cognitive trust management strategies give advantage even in environments with a high level of information noise. The results of the study are presented as follows. In Sect. 2 we consider details of multi-agent modeling for trust management in software freelance. Section 3 contains description of a NetLogo model for evaluating efficiency of different trust-management strategies. In Sect. 4 we analyze experimental results. Section 5 contain discussion topics and conclusion.

2 Issues of Multi-agent Trust in Relation to the Field of Freelance

Throughout history people cooperate with each other in different ways and under different conditions, they do it to perform different tasks and achieve different goals. At the same time the basis of cooperation in most cases is trust. Trust is not just a social attitude: it can also be applied for machines, tools and functional objects. Trust can be placed in processes or technologies, regarding their reliability and predictability, efficiency and friendliness.

Issues of trust become fundamental in open multi-agent systems (MAS), in which agents (both human and artificial agents) can enter and leave the system freely. Multi-agent systems have found their application in a wide variety of areas of human activity, such as in modeling social structures, ecological systems and transport communications, in robotics and computer games, in knowledge management systems and mobile technologies [12].

The delegation strategy is the rule that an agent-trustor uses to choose an agent-trustee to whom the task will be delegated. Strategy is the variable that we manipulate in experiments to evaluate which trustor performs better. Trust is a multi-layered concept and an important part of the conceptual core is trust as an action, as a decision to rely, depend on a trustee and delegate a task to him.

One of the key characteristics of agents in MAS is autonomy, i.e. the ability to perform most tasks without direct intervention from humans or other agents. Advances in technology lead to increased autonomy and complexity of agents and involve complex interactions and collaborations. Increased autonomy and complexity lead to increased human uncertainty and risks [18]. The only way to deal with someone else's autonomy is to establish truly trusting relationships.

A characteristic example of a multi-agent system is a freelance exchange. Trustors place orders which can relate to a variety of areas (for example, programming, design, copywriting), receive applications from potential performers who are ready and able to fulfill these orders, evaluate applications and select the most suitable agent. Sources of information in this case include direct experience of interaction with a trustee agent, his rating (reflecting the number or value of completed orders), reviews from other agents, third-party certificates (for example, educational documents), etc.

When considering a freelance exchange, parallels can be drawn between it and an e-commerce site: in both cases, interaction takes place online, a transaction takes place in which a product (e-commerce) or service (freelance) is sold. It was the models used on e-commerce sites (eBay, Amazon) that were among the first in the field of reputation and trust [13]. However, these models have a number of disadvantages: firstly, they are models of reputation, not trust (reputation should be considered as an important, but not the only condition for the emergence of trust), and secondly, they are centralized (each user has his own reputation profile stored in a centralized database).

It should be noted that modeling the mechanism for generating agent's trust assessments on a freelance exchange is still a problem. Using an adequate model for achieving trust will improve the efficiency of the functioning of both individual agents and the exchange as a whole.

Attempts to analyze, compare and classify existing models of trust and reputation have received considerable attention in the scientific literature. Examples of such reviews are the articles by Pinyol and Sabater-Mir [13], Sabater and Sierra [14], Balke [1], chapter 3 of Urbano's doctoral dissertation [20] and chapter 12 of Castelfranchi and Falcone's book [4]. Some of the most well-known trust models will be briefly discussed below. It should be noted that most of the models under consideration are close to the principles of multi-agent systems: in all models (except for the online-reputation and SPORAS models) the absence of a central arbiter is assumed, i.e. information about trust assessments is stored distributedly. In addition, the authors emphasize the autonomy of agents.

2.1 The Marsh Model

The Marsh model is one of the first computational models of trust presented in the literature and takes into account only direct experience [10]. The model defines three types of trust: basic (the trust disposition of agent x at time t), general (the trust that agent x has on agent y at time t without reference to a specific situation) and situational (the trust of agent x on agent y in the situation α). The author suggests three ways to calculate the overall trust score: the mean, minimum and maximum value from all available experience.

2.2 Models of Online Reputation

This type of models has been used on e-commerce sites (eBay, Amazon). Buyers purchase goods from sellers, after the transaction is completed, the buyer has the opportunity to evaluate the seller (in the eBay model three ratings are possible: positive (+1), neutral (0) and negative (−1)). The sum of all scores represents the reputation value, which is publicly available. Such systems are simple to implement and intuitive, but have reliability problems, do not consider false information and fraud and do not take into account the time aspect (a seller with high reputation value may begin to act as a bad one, but his actions will not have an immediate impact on reputation value).

2.3 Model SPORAS

This model uses the function of updating the reputation value of a trustee after receiving a new assessment [1]. The inputs to this function are the last reputation value of the trustee, the reputation of the user giving the rating and the rating itself. The model has the following features:

- new users start with a minimum reputation value and increase it with active interactions;
- the reputation value of an rated user cannot fall below the reputation value of a new user;
- if two users interact more than once, the system stores the last submitted rating;

- users with high reputation scores experience much smaller changes after each update than users with low reputation scores;
- the most recent ratings carry more weight in assessing a particular user's reputation.

In addition, the model contains a measure of the reliability of reputation assessment based on the deviation of reputation estimates: high deviations indicate a high degree of variability of reputation (or insufficiently active interaction of the user with others). Thus, there is an indicator of the predictive power of the algorithm.

2.4 Model Regret

In this model impressions are aggregated to calculate the reputation of trustee [14]. An impression captures the interaction between two agents from the point of view of the trustor and in relation to some aspect of the interaction. The trustor (agent a) stores a base of impressions about the trustee (agent b), on the basis of which he can evaluate the reputation obtained from direct experience (Ra → b), the reputation obtained from the direct experience of the group of agents A, which includes a (RA → b), the reputation based on trusted group B's experiences with agent b (RB → b), and the reputation derived from interactions between groups (RA → B). Each of these reputation values is calculated using a weighted average, where the weight is a function of the recency of the impression, giving more relevance to recent impressions. Aggregation of reputation values into a reputation score for one aspect of interaction also occurs using a weighted average formula, with weights selected according to the specific domain being assessed. The final measure of a trustee's reputation in one particular scenario is the aggregate of the reputations calculated for the various aspects of the interaction that make up that scenario. For this purpose, ontological graph structures are used.

2.5 FIRE Model

This model is in many ways similar to the Regret model. A fundamentally new source of trust in the model (along with direct experience and witness information) are certified reports – assessments provided by the assessed agent about himself and received from his partners during past interactions. The authors of the model view these assessments as something similar to letters of recommendation for employment [8]. The FIRE model also addresses a specific aspect of social trust – trust that arises from a role-based relationship between two agents. Each agent has a set of domain-specific rules, defined by the owner, that encode the norms of the environment. Such rules are hard-coded by the agent developer and lack the necessary flexibility in dynamic multi-agent systems. The main problem with the model is the assumption that agents are honest when exchanging information with each other. Obviously, reliability measures are needed for witness ratings and certified reports.

2.6 HABIT Model

HABIT model is a probabilistic model [20]. In this model, the vector of parameters $\theta_{tr \to te}$ is specified for each trustor/trustee pair, defining a distribution that represents the trustee's likely behavior during interactions with the trustor. Each truster/trustee pair has a belief model, which is the probability distribution $p(O_{tr \to te}|\theta_{tr \to te})$ of all observations $O_{tr \to te}$, where $p(O_{tr \to te})$ is a probability measure for all possible outcomes of interaction between the trustor and the trustee. Another component of HABIT is the reputation model. The trustor makes an inference about a particular fiduciary based on observations of any fiduciary obtained from any source (directly or from third parties). This means that the model can be used to predict the behavior of a trustee based on the behavior of groups of other agents. The authors of the model propose dividing agents into groups with similar behavior (for example, using cluster algorithms) and using a separate reputation model for each group.

2.7 Castelfranchi and Falcone's Socio-Cognitive Model

Within the framework of Castelfranchi and Falcone's socio-cognitive model [4] trust is a relational construct that links the following five components: agent X (trustor); agent Y (trustee); task of the trustee τ (action α of the trustee, which will possibly lead to a result p corresponding to the goal of the trustor); the goal of the trustor g_X; context, situation or environment C. Thus, the trustor X trusts in the trustee Y in context C to perform action α (executing task τ) that will lead to an outcome p (including or consistent with the trustor's goal g_X). The authors consider trust as a multi-level concept that includes the following layers: trust attitude, decision to trust, act of trusting, subsequent social interaction and trustor-trustee relationships.

Schematically socio-cognitive model of trust can be represented as a set of beliefs that lead to the decision to trust. Castelfranchi and Falcone use a fuzzy approach to implement their socio-cognitive model, in particular Fuzzy Cognitive Maps (FCM). Each belief is formed from sources; within the framework of the implementation of the model, four possible types of sources of beliefs are considered: direct experience, categorization, reasoning, reputation. The FCM has several nodes representing causal concepts (sources of belief, etc.) and edges representing the influence of the nodes on each other. The values of the nodes representing belief sources and the values of all edges are assigned by humans. These values are propagated through the FCM until a steady state is reached. The value of the nodes ranges from -1 (true negative) to $+1$ (true positive), this number represents the value of an individual trust attribute, obtained by combining the belief's confidence value (degree of confidence) and the score for that attribute. Some nodes receive input values from other nodes. Edges represent fuzzy rules or partial cause-and-effect relationships between concepts, with the edge sign ($+$ or $-$) indicating increase or decrease. Edge weight refers to the influence that one concept has on another.

2.8 SOLUM Model

SOLUM model was developed by J. Urbano in her doctoral dissertation A Situation-aware and Social Computational Trust Model [20]. The model consists of two parts: a general computational trust structure consisting of various evaluation functions and a set of computational components designed as possible implementations of the specified evaluation functions. The following are the design features of the model, which are based on the hypotheses put forward by the author:

- benevolence was included in the model;
- taking into account contextual information in the model, an approach with an emphasis on patterns of past behavior of trustee;
- integrity was included in the model.

The general structure of the SOLUM model consists of individual functions that allow you to evaluate:

1. The ability ($A_{x,y}$), integrity ($I_{x,y}$) and benevolence ($B_{x,y}$) of the assessed trustee.
2. The trustworthiness ($Tw_{x,y}$) of the trustee based on the aspects listed earlier.
3. The trust ($Tr_{x,y}$) of the trustor in relation to the trustee based on trustworthiness and other factors.

SOLUM model is in many ways an ideological successor to the approach of Castelfranchi and Falcone, within which the multidimensionality of trust was considered. However, their model assumed the existence of specific and detailed information about each of the dimensions of trust. The author of SOLUM suggests that in open and dynamic systems detailed information about the abilities, integrity and benevolence of specific trustees is not readily available. Therefore, the model uses computational components (Sinalpha, Contextual Fitness, Integrity Tuner and Social Tuner) capable of extracting relevant information from an available structured set of evidence. The model takes context into account and extracts trends in trustees' past behavior in various situations.

2.9 SIoT Model

Another trust model is discussed in the article A Bidirectional Trust Model for Service Delegation in Social Internet of Things (SIoT) [22]. Objects in SIoT can establish social relationships without human intervention, which improves the efficiency of interaction between objects and, as a result, the efficiency of service delivery. Each object in SIoT (smartphone, video camera, smart sensor) can be a service requester (SR) or service provider (SP) according to one's own motives. The SR broadcasts a service request (e.g., collecting urban noise data) and provides a reward to SP. In turn, the SP provides a specific service (exchange of information or computing resources) for the SR to receive a reward. Objects in SIoT can autonomously determine which service to initiate and which object to delegate a task to within a set of candidate objects.

In contrast to the unidirectional approach that has become traditional in the literature (when only the SR's need to assess trust in the SP is taken into account), the authors of the article propose a bidirectional model for assessing and selecting SR and SP, designed to prevent their harmful behavior. The model is context-sensitive, i.e. takes into account the properties of the task in a specific environment. Trust assessment is based on opinion and evidence and uses subjective logic to determine its quantitative value. In addition, the correlation between trust and utility and their impact on service delegation is examined. The model uses a number of simplifications, in particular, the composition of evidence includes only service attributes, information about bidirectional service evaluations, service time, etc. without taking into account the relationships between the characteristics of devices of SIoT objects and the properties of the service. Accordingly, the model is more suitable for scenarios where the degree of heterogeneity and differentiation of SIoT devices is low.

The review of existing trust models resulted in a comparative table (Table 1). The following classification criteria were chosen:

1. Type of paradigm: mathematical (game theoretical approaches, trust/reputation is considered as a subjective probability) or cognitive (cognitive aspects are included).
2. Context: single-context (trust in the model is associated with a specific context) or multi-context model.
3. Information visibility: trust/reputation information can be considered a global property that can be observed by all other agents, or a subjective/private property that each agent creates.
4. Positioning: trust model or reputation model.

Table 1. Alternatives for formalization of trust management

Model	Paradigm	Context	Visibility	Positioning
Marsh	Mathematic	Multiple	Subjective	Trust
eBay, Amazon	Mathematic	Single	Global	Reputation
SPORAS	Mathematic	Single	Global	Reputation
Regret	Mathematic	Multiple	Subjective	Trust, Rep
FIRE	Mathematic	Multiple	Subjective	Trust, Rep
HABIT	Mathematic	Multiple	Global	Trust, Rep
Castelfranchi and Falcone	Cognitive/M	Multiple	Subjective	Trust
SOLUM	Cognitive/M	Single	Global	Trust
Bidirectional Trust Model (SIoT)	Cognitive/M	Single	Global	Trust

3 Structure of the Freelance Exchange Simulation Model

The freelance exchange simulation model is based on Castelfranchi and Falcone's socio-cognitive model of trust, which is presented in their book [4]. The model is the result of many years of research, it is well founded and rich, and the authors' theory of trust includes detailed discussions about the sources of beliefs and the nature of trust. Modeling was carried out using NetLogo, which is both an agent-oriented language for developing models and systems and an integrated modeling environment [11].

Within the freelance exchange model, six agents are considered: one trustor and five potential trustees. There is also a set of 100 tasks, each task belongs to one of three types (design, programming or copywriting) and has a certain level of difficulty. Trustees, in turn, are characterized by abilities (their meaning differs for each type of task) and level of willingness (reflects involvement in the task and does not depend on the type of task being performed). It is supposed that there is no cheating in the model: only those agents whose abilities allow them to complete a task of a given level of difficulty submit applications for performance. Besides it, a dynamic environment is considered, which can both complicate and simplify the task. The trustor is able to choose a strategy for delegating tasks; four different strategies are considered within the framework of the model:

- a trustor who acts randomly;
- a trustor who acts on the basis of statistics;
- a cognitive trustor;
- a cognitive trustor whose trust assessments are subject to errors (noise).

The operating algorithm of the simulation model includes the following steps:

1. Description and creation of agents (the trustor and five trustees) with specified characteristics.
2. Description and creation of a set of 100 tasks, each task belongs to one of three types (design, programming, copywriting) and has a certain level of difficulty. The set of tasks is the same for any run of the model; this is done to ensure comparability of experimental results.
3. Creation of a changing environment (re-simulated at each tick of the model).
4. Selecting a random task from the general set. This task will need to be performed on the current tick of the model.
5. Selection of agents capable of completing it (comparing their abilities with the difficulty of the current task). Formation of a pool of such agents. If no agent is potentially capable of completing the task, this task is destroyed, then movement to step 3.
6. The trustor's choice of one of four possible delegation strategies.
7. Selection of a specific trustee agent.
8. The process of completing a task that ends in success or failure. Deleting the task, updating the characteristics of the agents and the statistical characteristics of the model.
9. Movement to step three.
10. Stopping of the model if there are no tasks left.

The model development process will be discussed in more detail next. The first two steps of the algorithm include the description and creation of agents. Trustors have only one property, credit, which reflects the number of successfully completed tasks. Trustees have a whole set of properties, which include:

- abilities (*ability_1, ability_2, ability_3*) – agent skills for performing various types of tasks. Real numbers from 0 to 1 are assigned randomly when the model is run;
- willingness (*willingness*) – reflects the agent's involvement in completing the task (how many resources or time he will spend). This property reflects the fact that even an experienced agent can fail if it does not use enough resources. A real number from 0 to 1, is set randomly when running the model;

- environment (*environment*) – reflects the state of the environment. The color of the patch on which the agent is located is determined, then the color value is reduced to a number in the interval $(-1, 1)$;
- number of tasks delegated to the agent (*num_deleg_tasks*);
- number of tasks completed by the agent (*num_compl_tasks*);
- ratio of completed and delegated tasks, percentage of completion (*stat_tasks*);
- trust assessments by the cognitive trustor (*trust_cogn_1, trust_cogn_2, trust_cogn_3*) – it is supposed that the trustor knows true information about the agent's abilities and willingness, as well as about the environment in which the task will be performed. Trust scores are modeled as functions of the specified properties, with the base weights of nodes and edges of the graph taken from the [2]. The model provides levers (*weight_ability, weight_willing, weight_environ, weight_internal, weight_external*) that allow changing these weights.
- distorted trust assessments (*trust_cogn_noise_1, trust_cogn_noise_2, trust_cogn_noise_3*) – it is assumed that the trustor's knowledge contains errors. Errors are modeled as noise, a deviation from the true value of the trust assessment estimated by a certain percentage. The model has a lever (*noise_level*), which allows setting the noise level.

The tasks in the model have two properties: class, reflecting their type (1 – design, 2 – programming, 3 – copywriting), and difficulty_level, containing the level of difficulty (a real number from 0 to 1).

The model at the moment of initialization is shown in Fig. 1. A trustor (yellow person), trustees (red persons) and tasks (boxes, color depends on the type of task) are created. It should be noted that the set of tasks in all runs of the model remains the same: 12 tasks of the first type with a difficulty level of 0,2 (easy), 11 tasks of the first type with a difficulty level of 0,5 (medium), 11 tasks of the first type with a level difficulty 0,8 (hard), 11 tasks of the second type with a difficulty level of 0,2 (easy), etc.

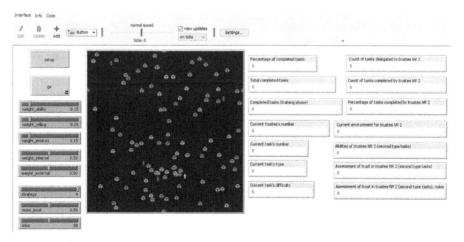

Fig. 1. The model at the moment of initialization (Color figure online)

In the third step of the algorithm the environment is created using the setup-patches function. The patch color *pcolor* is specified as a random number from 0 (black) to 9,99 (white). Therefore, the darker the environment, the stronger its negative impact on the agent's task performance. As already mentioned, the environment is generated anew at each step of the model. The fourth step, selecting a random task from the set, is implemented using the task-selection function. In this case, the agent number, task type and difficulty are transferred to global variables.

At the fifth step agents are capable of completing the task are selected. If the agent's ability value is greater than the difficulty of the task, then agent changes color from red to green – the submission of applications by trustees is simulated. There is no cheating in the model, so agents with insufficient abilities cannot apply submission. It should be noted that if none of the agents is able to complete the task, it is destroyed and the model moves on to the next step (this mechanism is implemented within the *go* function).

In the sixth and seventh steps a delegation strategy is selected and a specific task performer is determined. The model implements the *strategy-choice* function for selecting a delegation strategy; the choice depends on the value of the global variable *strategy*, which is set using the corresponding lever. As part of the experiments, it is assumed that the tasks are not related to each other and are not part of the same project, so a random order of task selection is acceptable. Let's take a closer look at each of the delegation strategies:

1. A trustor who acts randomly. A random trustee is selected from among the agents who submitted applications. The global variable *trustee_num* stores the number of this agent.
2. A trustor who acts on the basis of statistics. In this case, there is a training phase, during which some tasks are delegated (their number is determined by the global variable *educ*; a lever is provided in the model to regulate this variable), the remaining tasks are delegated during the experiment phase. As an element of the training phase, the trustor delegates tasks one by one to all agents who submitted applications (it is implemented by selecting an agent with a minimum number of delegated tasks). In the experiment phase, the trustor selects agents with the best *stat_tasks* indicator, i.e. percentage of completed tasks. It does not take into account the agent's abilities and willingness, nor the state of the environment, only learning based on direct interaction. When calculating the percentage of completed tasks, only those that were delegated during the experiment phase are taken into account.
3. A cognitive trustor. The trustor knows a priori the properties of all agents and the state of the environment in which they are located; there is no training. The agent with the maximum trust score value is selected (*trust_cogn_1, trust_cogn_2* or *trust_cogn_3* depending on the type of task).
4. A cognitive trustor whose trust assessments are subject to errors (noise). This strategy allows bringing the model closer to a more realistic one. The strategy is similar to the previous one, only the choice here is made based on the adjusted trust score (*trust_cogn_noise_1, trust_cogn_noise_2, trust_cogn_noise_3*). The noise level (possible percentage deviation of the estimate) is set using the *noise_level* lever. And the correction of trust scores itself is carried out within the go function.

The eighth step is to complete the task, which can either be successful or vice versa. To complete the task agent needs to score three hits (*hit*). A hit is scored if the random number rolled (from 0 to 1) is less than the sum of the agent's ability (from 0 to 1) and the environment (from −1 to 1). The number of try (*try*) attempts is defined as ten times the agent's willingness, rounded up to the nearest whole number. If completing the task is successful, the cred variable is increased by one, i.e. the trustor receives 1 credit for a successfully completed task. The num_compl_tasks property, which contains the number of tasks completed by the agent, is also increased by one. Regardless of the success of execution, the task is destroyed at the end of the process. After the hundredth tick, when all tasks are destroyed, the model completes its work.

The simulation model during operation is shown in Fig. 2. There are levers responsible for the weights when calculating the trust assessment, a lever for choosing a strategy, a lever for the noise level in the model, as well as a lever that determines the number of tasks in the training phase (for strategy 2) on the left side. There are various monitors showing percentage of completed tasks, total number of completed tasks and number of tasks completed in the training phase (for strategy 2), characteristics of the current task (it is executed on the current tick), as well as a number of properties of trustee № 2 on the right side.

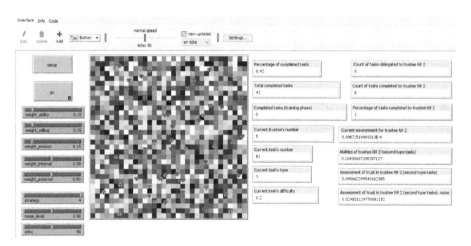

Fig. 2. Model during operation, tick 50

The constructed simulation model complies with the principles of multi-agency: the behavior of agents is autonomous, there is no central arbiter in the model and information about trust assessments is stored in a distributed way.

4   Experimental Study of the Model

As an element of the study of the model, a number of experiments were carried out, the main purpose of which was to compare the results when using each of the delegation strategies. In the first experiment 500 runs of the model are performed with the trustor using strategy 1 (random selection of a trustee from among those capable of completing the task). Strategy 1 is considered as basic and is needed mainly for comparison with other delegation strategies. The received data was processed in Excel, the average value of the percentage of completed tasks was determined and made up 34,38%.

In the second experiment, the trustor uses strategy 2 (acts on the basis of statistics, selects the trustee with the maximum ratio of the number of tasks completed to the number of delegated tasks). In this case, the variable *educ* varies, which is responsible for the number of tasks used in the training phase. Three options are considered: 0 tasks (there is no training phase actually), 30 and 50 tasks. The experiment shows that even in the absence of training (0 tasks), the statistical trustor shows better results than random ones: 47,57% versus 34,38%. When the number of tasks in the training phase increases to 30, the percentage of completed tasks increases to 52,56%, which indicates the effectiveness of training. However, a further increase in the number of tasks in the training phase does not lead to a significant improvement in performance: with 50 tasks in the training set, the percentage of completed tasks is 52,66%. Therefore, for further comparison of strategies, we will use a version of the strategy with training on 30 tasks as a statistical one.

The third experiment demonstrates the trustor's use of strategy 3, i.e. the trustor is cognitive, knows the true values of the agents' abilities and willingness, as well as the state of the environment. The average percentage of completed tasks is 75,44%, which is significantly higher than both random and statistical trustors. Such a high result indicates the superiority of the cognitive strategy.

The fourth experiment examines the use of strategy 4 (cognitive trustor, trust assessments are subject to errors, in the model errors are generated as noise using the *noise_level* variable). In this case, the *noise_level* value varies and is 0,1, 0,2, 0,4 or 0,5 (accordingly, the trust assessment contains an error of 10, 20, 40 or 50%). As a result of the experiment, a completely logical conclusion was obtained: the higher the noise level, the lower the average percentage of tasks completed. It is important to note that even with an error level of 50%, the cognitive strategy is superior to the statistical one: the average percentage of completed tasks here is 62,86% (versus 52,56% for the statistical one).

The results of all experiments are combined and presented in a bar graph (Fig. 3). As already mentioned, the best result in terms of the average percentage of completed tasks was shown by strategy 3, corresponding to the cognitive trustor (Cognitive). Moreover, even if trust assessments are subject to distortions (due to inaccurate information and errors), cognitive strategies still show better results than statistical ones. The results obtained are generally consistent with the results of the experiments of [2].

The created simulation model made it possible to demonstrate the advantages of the socio-cognitive approach in relation to the statistical one. A comparative analysis of two concepts of trust was carried out:

1. The concept of a «statistical trustor»: based on the assumption that it is possible to model trust in agents only on the basis of direct experience with them (which can be positive or negative). In fact, only one dimension is taken into account here: the number of successes or failures of agents in previous steps.

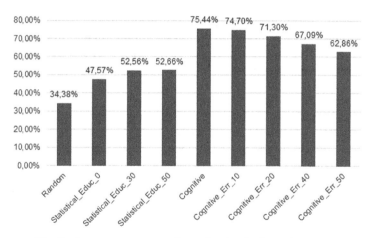

Fig. 3. Average percentage of completed tasks for each strategy

2. The concept of a «cognitive trustor»: based on consideration of a whole combination of factors. These factors must be considered before trusting an agent (it includes both the properties of the trustee and the properties of the environment).

5 Conclusion

In this study we applied a technique of multi-agent simulation for evaluation of different strategies for trust management. Trust management of autonomous entities becomes a critical aspect in modern business especially in the context of Industry 5.0. The sharing economy, the concept emerging in the frame of Industry 5.0 has any number of ingredients, characteristics or descriptors: technology enabled, preference for access over ownership, peer to peer, sharing of personal assets (versus corporate assets), ease of access, increased social interaction, collaborative consumption and openly shared user feedback (resulting in increased trust). Not all are present in every "sharing economy" transaction. Most companies profess to be collaborative, but their claims will be tested as real-time data and analytics are applied to the way they target and serve their customers. The digital age is about accessing and using data, refining the products and experiences, and moving to a world of continual adjustment and refinement while ensuring that the human dimension of the interaction remains at the heart of the process. Focusing on these business ingredients requires design of new approaches for trust management.

Different sources [15, 23] underline that the concept of Industry 5.0 as a subsequent phase of Industry 4.0 is centred around values, such as human-centricity, ecological or social benefits. This paradigm shift is based on the idea that technologies can be shaped towards supporting values. This is especially important as ongoing societal developments in the fourth industrial revolution change the way value is created, exchanged and distributed [17]. The technologies at the core of Industry 5.0 are largely congruent with Industry 4.0, while a stronger focus on human-centred technologies and, hence, cooperation problems forms the basis for Industry 5.0.

In that context our experimental results showed that in all cases cognitive trustors performed better than statistical ones in terms of overall success (number of credits gained). Thus, the cognitive strategy more effectively models agents and characteristics of the environment and also allows for the allocation of resources with high accuracy. The superiority of the cognitive agent over the statistical agent is maintained even in those experiments where the knowledge of the cognitive agent is noisy. In contrast, even with an increase in the amount of data during the training phase the statistical trustor does not show a significant increase in efficiency.

The model is at an early stage of development. In the future it is planned to include empirical data in it. Besides, the model does not capture for now certain unpredictable human factors, competitive business strategies, or market fluctuations, possibly over-simplifying the trust dynamics in real-world business environment. Next, we outline a number of problematic questions, the search for answers to which can be the basis for further research. These questions include:

1. Modeling the trust evaluation function. In [4] the fuzzy cognitive maps are used as part of their model. It makes sense to study other approaches to building a trust function in more detail.
2. Connected to the previous issue is the transformation of information/beliefs obtained from sources into quantitative assessments of the characteristics of trustees. For example, the source of information about the abilities of an agent on a freelance exchange can be documents about the received education (from trusted third parties). And the source of information about its willingness is the ratings/reviews of other agents. However, bringing this information into a form that can be used in a simulation model is a difficult task in itself.
3. Implementation of barriers and threshold values into the model. For example, if an agent has sufficient ability to perform a task, but his willingness is below a threshold, the trustor will not consider such an agent as a potential performer.
4. Enrichment of the model and bringing it closer to reality by more accurately modeling external factors. Among them adding time and money plays a special role. Time can be included in the model in several ways: firstly, as the duration of the task, and secondly, as a limited duration of waiting for applications from agents. The model does not consider money, but this aspect also deserves attention. For example, we can add to the model the cost of each task (which the trustor receives upon its successful completion), service prices of trustees (depending on their abilities). In addition, it will allow us to model a trustor who seeks to maximize his profit.

Last but not least, the modeling approach proposed also requires methodological improvements in tooling and generalization aspects. Any particular simulation tool brings own limitations and accents, so our next modeling efforts should be focused on reproducing similar trust phenomena within different paradigms of multi-agent simulations (like BDI-based Jason framework). We believe that generalization of the results across several simulation approaches and application domains will aim at producing reliable foundations of computationally tractable and socially accepted algorithms for trust management in realities of Industry 5.0.

Primarily, we are focused on operationalizing trust management in the form of computationally tractable multi-agent algorithms. As a result of our work, organizational engineering receives an algorithmic artifact (a multi-agent algorithm) that demonstrates advantages over other methods and can be integrated into management and planning systems. Obtaining new knowledge specifically in the aspect of socio-cognitive research (i.e., the development of trust management theory itself) is the next step.

References

1. Balke, T., Knig, S., Torsten, E.: A survey on reputation systems for artificial societies. Technical Report. Bayreuth University, vol. 46 (2009)
2. Blazhchuk, N., Malyzhenkov, P., Masi, M.: Organizational structure reengineering based on the transaction approach: case of construction business. In: CAiSE 2021 International Workshops Melbourne, VIC, Australia, June 28 – July 2, 2021 Proceedings, Lecture Notes in Business Information Processing, 423, Springer Nature Switzerland AG (2021)
3. Cardoni, A.: Business planning and management accounting in strategic networks: theoretical development and empirical evidence from enterprises' network "agreement". Management Control 3 (2012)
4. Castelfranchi, C., Falcone, R.: Trust Theory: A Socio-Cognitive and Computational Model // Wiley Series in Agent Technology. John Wiley & Sons Ltd., Chichester, 369 p. (2010)
5. Castells, M.: The Rise of the Network Society. Blackwell Publishers, Oxford (2000)
6. Hakansson, H., Ford, D., Gadde, L.E., Shenota, I., Waluszewski, A.: Business in Networks. John Wiley & Sons Ltd, New York (2010)
7. Huggins, R.: Forms of network resource: knowledge access and the role of inter-firm networks. Int. J. Manage. Rev. 12(3), 335–352 (2010)
8. Huynh, T., Jennings, N., Shadbolt, N.: An integrated trust and reputation model for open multi-agent systems. Autonomous Agents and Multi-Agent Systems, vol. 13, pp. 119–154 (2006)
9. Johanson, M., Lundberg, H.: Network Strategies for Regional Growth. Palgrave MacMillan (2011)
10. Marsh, S.: Formalising trust as a computational concept. Ph.D. thesis, Department of Mathematics and Computer Science, University of Stirling (1994)
11. Mezentsev, K.N.: Multi-agent modeling in the NetLogo environment. Saint Petersburg: Izdatel'stvo Lan', 176 p. (2015)
12. Ossowski, S., Sierra, C., Botti, V.: Agreement Technologies: A Computing Perspective. In: Agreement Technologies. Law, Governance and Technology Series, vol. 8, pp. 3–16 (2013)
13. Pinyol, I., Sabater-Mir, J.: Computational trust and reputation models for open multi-agent systems: a review. Artif. Intell. Rev. **40**, 1–25 (2013)
14. Sabater, J., Sierra, C.: Review on computational trust and reputation models. Artif. Intell. Rev. **24**, 33–60 (2005)
15. Saniuk, S., Grabowska, S., Straka, M.: Identification of social and economic expectations: contextual reasons for the transformation process of industry 4.0 into the industry 5.0 concept. Sustainability, 14(3) (2022)
16. Scapens, R., W., Varoutsa, E.: Accounting in inter-organisational relationships – the institutional theory perspective. In: Hakansson, H., Krauss, K., Lind, J.: Accounting in Networks. Routledge, London (2010)
17. Schwab, K.: The Fourth Industrial Revolution. World Economic Forum (2016)
18. Such, J.: Attacks and vulnerabilities of trust and reputation models. In: Agreement Technologies. Law, Governance and Technology Series, vol. 8, 467–477 (2013)
19. Tomkins, C.: Interdependencies, trust and information in relationship, alliances and networks. Acc. Organ. Soc. **26**, 161–191 (2001)

20. Urbano, J.: A Situation-aware and Social Computational Trust Model. Doctoral dissertation, Faculty of Engineering, University of Porto (2013)
21. Vitro, R., A.: The knowledge economy in development: perspectives for effective partnerships. Washington, D.C (2005); Williamson, O., E.: Market and Hierarchies. Free Press, New York (1975)
22. Wei, L., Yang, Y., Wu, J., Long, C., Lin, Y-B.: A bidirectional trust model for service delegation in social internet of things. Future Internet. **14,** 135–151 (2022)
23. Xu, X., Lu, Y., Vogel-Heuser, B., Wang, L.: Industry 4.0 and Industry 5.0 - Inception, conception and perception. J. Manuf. Syst. **61** (2020)

Ontological Analysis of Dimensional Modeling Concepts in Data Warehousing/Business Intelligence Systems

Petr Prokop(✉)⬛ and Robert Pergl⬛

Faculty of Information Technology, Czech Technical University in Prague, Prague,
Czech Republic
{prokope3,robert.pergl}@fit.cvut.cz

Abstract. Collecting, processing and utilizing data information plays an increasingly important role in data warehousing/business intelligence (DWH/BI) systems. Currently, these systems are predominantly described using natural text, informal diagrams, or UML (Unified Modeling Language) diagrams. These potentially imprecise methods for describing new or complex DWH/BI topics can in combination with variations in naming and interpretations of concepts between different authors lead to miscommunication issues. This paper shows the possibility and benefits of using a more formal approach in documenting and describing such systems or their parts, which results in a more precise form of communication between researchers or industry experts. The conceptual analysis of selected parts of the DWH/BI domain is done using the OntoUML modeling language.

Keywords: dimensional modeling · data warehouse · business intelligence · DWH/BI · ontological analysis · conceptual modeling · OntoUML

1 Introduction

Value of data and possible insights extracted from this data was well known to companies even in the nineteenth century, when the term business intelligence was coined for the first time in [1].

As we entered the age of information [2], not long after the invention of the transistor in 1947, the field of BI moved into the domain of digital information systems, which led to an exponential increase in the collected and processed data and the value of insights gained from the collected data is increasing to this date [3–5].

Hence, a strong need for a reliable methodology for the documentation, construction, and maintenance of this type of systems occurred. Currently, mostly free text, informal graphical models, and UML models are usually used for description of DWH/BI systems and related concepts. All these techniques for

© The Author(s), under exclusive license to Springer Nature Switzerland AG 2024
M. Malinova Mandelburger et al. (Eds.): EDEWC 2023, LNBIP 510, pp. 35–51, 2024.
https://doi.org/10.1007/978-3-031-58935-5_3

DWH/BI system description are prone to vague and ambiguous descriptions, which in turn could lead to miscommunication between researchers or IT professionals resulting in DWH/BI projects delays or budget overruns.

1.1 Research Goals

The objective of this article is to explore the feasibility and impact of applying formal ontological analysis through OntoUML within the Data Warehousing/Business Intelligence (DWH/BI) domain. The aim is to ascertain OntoUML's potential in enhancing the ontological precision of dimensional modeling's core concepts, both for academic exploration and practical deployments. Our research seeks to explore how OntoUML's structured and theoretically well-founded approach to modeling can potentially contribute to clarifying and refining the foundational elements of DWH/BI, thus potentially driving advancements in the domain's research methodologies or its application in real-world scenarios.

1.2 Methodology

Key concepts are identified and selected from the DWH/BI domain, modeled using the OntoUML language, and then compared with the results obtained by commonly used methods. The criterion for the comparison of our results is ontological clarity of conceptualization, which can be guaranteed by proper usage of a theoretically well-founded modeling language (such as OntoUML) and proper tools, which can help enforce the adherence to OntoUML rules.

The rest of the paper is structured as follows: Sect. 2 summarizes related work, Sect. 3 introduces key relevant concepts from DWH/BI, Sect. 4 presents our approach to ontological analysis using the modeling language OntoUML, Sect. 5 presentation of our results, and finally Sect. 6 discusses our results and possibilities for further research.

2 Related Work

To the best of our knowledge, there is currently no work related to ontological analysis of dimensional modeling concepts within DWH/BI domain, the closest works focus on comparisons of the main approaches to designing DWH/BI systems, modeling of ETL (Extract-Transform-Load) processes, and modeling the process of dimensional modeling.

The authors of [17] present an extensive literature review of modeling methods for ETL processes. They split current ETL modeling approaches into six categories – UML, ontology, MDA (Model-Driven Architecture), graphical, ad hoc formalisms, and approaches for Big Data. However, the reviewed approaches focus rather on the ETL workflow (i.e. steps of data transformation), technological aspects, conceptual modeling of business data and transformation between conceptual, logical, and physical models.

Furthermore, [10–13] authors introduce and present their original versions of the DWH/BI approaches.

In [14] the author describes an agile approach to dimensional modeling in a DWH/BI setting. This work mainly focuses on collecting business requirements and transforming them into dimensional schemas.

The authors in [18] conducted an analysis of differences between the main approaches to designing DWH/BI systems.

With the exception of works listed in [17], all mentioned authors use for description and comparison of DWH/BI domain natural language text, ad hoc notation, informal diagrams, E-R (Entity-Relationship) or UML diagrams.

On the other hand, there are numerous success stories published about using OntoUML to improve ontological clarification of various domains. We mention two notable examples here: In [15] the authors apply OntoUML in the domain of gas and oil extraction. As a result of the creation of the OntoUML model, the authors managed to improve the clarity of several key concepts within the gas and oil extraction industry. The other notable example is [16] where authors expand upon existing legal specific ontology called UFO-L and present the *right-duty relation* pattern for modeling concepts within the legal domain.

3   Theoretical Background

3.1   DWH/BI

Over the years, multiple authors have stated several definitions of terms BI and DWH, which naturally differ (even though the key ideas are usually the same). The definitions presented are those that suit the needs of this article the best.

Business Intelligence is a term independent of data warehouse – the concept of BI was well known and used even before the first electronic computers. The first recorded definition of BI is "ability to collect and react accordingly based on the information retrieved" and dates back to 1865 [1]. Modern definitions are refinements of the original, but the original idea holds to this date - BI is a process of collecting, processing and analyzing data for the purpose of optimizing business decisions.

Data warehouse is a system that is a type of decision support system [10,12] – its goal is to extract, clean and integrate data from multiple sources and deliver them to the end user for the purpose of decision making. In short, a data warehouse is an implementation of business intelligence functionality.

3.2   OntoUML

The OntoUML modeling language is an extension profile for UML and is based on a Unified Foundational Ontology (UFO), which is a type of formal ontology based on cognitive sciences and modal logic [6].

Currently, UFO-A, UFO-B, and UFO-C are the main parts of the UFO, each focused on different aspects of reality. UFO-A deals with static aspects, such as objects and their relationships. UFO-B addresses the dynamic aspects, covering events and changes over time. UFO-C explores social and intentional aspects, including agents, intentions, and social constructs. The main differences lie in their focus areas: UFO-A is about the structure of entities, UFO-B about temporal dynamics, and UFO-C about social interactions and intentions. More advances in UFO have been made through UFO-S [8] to provide a detailed explanation of services and related concepts, offering a commitment-based perspective on what constitutes a service.

In this article, we use only concepts from UFO-A, but discuss the possibility of application of UFO-B, UFO-C and UFO-S at the conclusion of this article.

In the field of informatics, formal ontology serves as a tool for better understanding, description, and representation of concepts, their properties, categories, and relationships between them. One of the commonly accepted definitions of formal ontology in informatics is: "An ontology is a formal and explicit specification of a shared conceptualization" [7].

Formal ontology itself has its roots in the philosophical discipline of ontology, which is the philosophy of organization and the nature of existence [9].

The goal of OntoUML is to provide a theoretically well-founded modeling language for a more subtle and precise conceptual modeling of the given problem domain.

In the rest of this section we introduce a necessary subset of OntoUML concepts used in this paper.

Rigidity. Rigidity is a concept rooted in modal logic and is used in ontology and OntoUML to denote the property of certain types of entity that remain the same over time. In OntoUML, a type is considered rigid if instances of it maintain their types through time. For example, a person remains a person throughout their life, and thus *Person* is a rigid type. Example of anti-rigid type are *Poor* and *Rich* phases of a *Person* as it is possible through time to oscillate between these two states.

Kind and Subkind. *Kind* is a foundational category that represents a rigid type of entity that provides identity and has inherent properties that are shared across all its instances throughout its existence. *Subkind* is a rigid specialization of a identity providing type, inheriting all properties of the supertype but having additional specific characteristics. For instance, *Female* or *Male* could be subkinds of the kind *Person*, adding gender-specific attributes.

Category. *Category* is a high-level or top-level abstraction used to group entities sharing common properties, but following different identity principles. They help to structure the ontology at a high level of abstraction, enabling better organization and understanding of the conceptual model.

Phase. A *Phase* refers to an anti-rigid specialization of an entity, marking different temporal conditions while the intrinsic nature of the entity remains unchanged. For instance, *Infancy* and *Adulthood* are phases in the human life-cycle, each with distinct characteristics.

Role. A *Role* is an anti-rigid specialization of an entity that can be temporarily assumed based on certain external conditions and specific relations. For example, a person can assume the role of a *Student* or *Employee* under different circumstances. A key difference between *Phase* and *Role* is, that *Role* is based on mandatory external relationship – e.g., for *Student* it could be relation with *University Enrollment* entity that makes this *Student* specialization valid.

Disjoint and Complete. In OntoUML, the meta-attributes *disjoint* and *complete* are used to describe the relationships and coverage between subtypes within the type hierarchy. *Disjoint* subtypes are mutually exclusive - an instance can belong to only one subtype at a time. *Complete* subtypes collectively cover all instances of the supertype, with no instance left unclassified. Both these attributes are specification of inheritance relation from UML Class diagrams.

Essential. The *essential* stereotype is applied to properties that inherently and necessarily characterize an individual of a given type, indicating that the property is fundamental to the existence and identification of the individual of that type. This stereotype helps to distinguish those characteristics that are absolutely necessary for an individual to be considered as an instance of a certain kind or to fulfill a specific role, from those that are merely accidental or contingent.

Specific usage of *essential* relation is for example between *Person* and *Brain* – identity and existence of every *Person* deeply interconnected with their exact *Brain*.

Inseparable. The *inseparable* stereotype describes relationships where related entities cannot exist independently of one another. This concept is used to denote a strong ontological dependency between entities, signifying that if one entity ceases to exist, the other must necessarily cease to exist as well. This relationship highlights fundamental and existential dependencies within the model, emphasizing the codependence of entities in certain contexts.

Specific usage of *inseparable* relation is for example between *Wall* and *Hole in the Wall* – if instance *Wall* ceases to exist, the instance of *Hole in the Wall* can not exist on its own.

Mode. *Mode* is a rigid and existentially dependent aspect that represents the intrinsic unstructured property of its bearer. As opposed to *Quality*, *Mode* is aspect that does not represent a directly measurable property.

Some examples of *Mode* include *Version* of a code, *Skill* of a person or *Financial Status* of a company.

Shareability. The concepts of composition and aggregation from UML are replaced by more precise and well defined concepts (e.g. *Collective* or *Quantity*). However, for purposes of syntactical compatibility between OntoUML and UML, OntoUML defines the symbol of empty diamond for *shareable* parts and full diamond for *non-shareable* parts. Although information about shareability of parts is already contained in the multiplicities of relations between parts and a whole.

3.3 Dimensional Modeling

Dimensional modeling is a data architecture framework commonly used in data warehousing and business intelligence to optimize databases for querying and reporting. Introduced and popularized by Ralph Kimball [12,19], the methodology centers around facts and dimensions, where facts are quantitative metrics (e.g., sales, revenue) and dimensions provide contextual details (e.g., time, location). Employing schemas like Star or Snowflake, dimensional modeling aims to enhance query performance and data retrieval by organizing data in a way that is intuitive and efficient for end-users.

3.4 Slowly Changing Dimension

Slowly Changing Dimension (SCD) is a type of dimensional table in a data warehouse that has attributes whose values change over time. SCDs are designed to manage and track these changes, allowing for historical data analysis, and most notably, they provide means to analyze business in both "as is" and "as was" fashion. The concept of SCD was originally described in [12] and then expanded in [19]. There are four basic types of SCD which can be summarized as:

- SCD 0: The attribute is not versioned or changed in any way. It is included for the completeness of categorization of SCDs and would result in an empty implementation.
- SCD 1: The attribute value is overwritten, and no history is kept.
- SCD 2: Historical values of the attribute are stored in separate records.
- SCD 3: Historical values are stored parallel to the current value, and they provide "alternative reality".

The rest of the commonly used SCDs (4, 5, 6 and 7) are either combination, optimization, or both of previously listed types (SCD 1-3).

4   Approach

Our goal is to apply the OntoUML modeling language on selected parts of the dimensional modeling within the DWH/BI domain.

First, we create a simple conceptual model using UML Class diagram, then we expand on that diagram through usage of OntoUML. This initial diagram was based on textual descriptions and informal diagrams of these concepts as presented by [3,12,14,19].

OntoUML through its richer and deeper semantics and grammar leads modellers' hand and gives "hints" on what to focus next; for example, it can help discover missing entities, attributes, or relations. Common questions we asked when we followed the OntoUML rules during our modeling efforts were following:

- Is this type/property rigid or anti-rigid?
- What is the identity source of this entity?
- Is this an abstract umbrella concept or a specific entity?
- Is this property based on external "truth-maker" or is it based on intrinsic attribute?
- If it is a subtype, did we include all subtypes? Can these subtypes overlap?

5 Results

During our modeling efforts, we created a conceptual model containing hundreds of entities and relations. In this section we present a small subset of created model that in our opinion showcases the benefits of application of OntoUML in the DWH/BI domain.

5.1 Initial UML Class Diagram

As the first step, we created a conceptual model of some fundamental concepts within the DWH/BI system, such as categorization of SCD types. The resulting diagram is shown in Fig. 1. This model serves as a starting point for our further work and will be significantly expanded by iterative application of OntoUML concepts and rules.

5.2 DWH Table Types

The initial UML conceptual model captures three types of basic subtypes of database tables in DWH/BI systems and one specialization of *Dimension* table, namely *SCD*. This table itself has a specific attribute called *Type* that represents the specific historization strategy of this table. This model also captures eight different types of SCD that are commonly recognized [19].

After applying OntoUML specific concepts on database types of tables, we arrived at the model presented in Fig. 2. The resulting model tells us a quite richer story about this hierarchy. First, *Dimension* and *Fact* follow different identity principles as their data sources and general roles within the system differ. Next, *Auxiliary* is modeled as *Category* as it is an abstract umbrella over a large number of tables that share similarities, but we cannot find a common identity principle at this point, and finding more subtypes is necessary.

Auxiliary tables would be typically used for tasks such as error handling, generation of surrogate keys, support for meta-data and data lineage, etc.

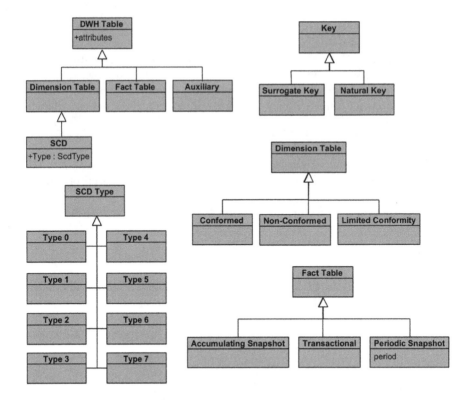

Fig. 1. Initial conceptual model using UML Class Diagram.

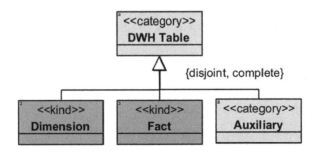

Fig. 2. Categorization of tables using OntoUML.

5.3   Technical and Domain Attributes

Next we focused on modeling attributes and their relationships. The resulting model is depicted in Fig. 3.

We decided to model *Attribute* as *Category* type as it encompasses common properties of both subtypes, most notably both subtypes have a data type and value. Both *Domain* and *Technical* attributes were modeled as *Kind* as both have a different source of identity. The source of identity for *Technical* attribute is

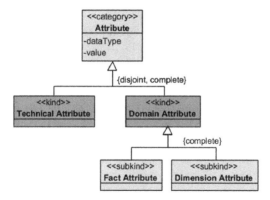

Fig. 3. OntoUML model of attributes and their relation to fact and dimension tables.

a specific ETL process that generated the said attribute. On the other hand, the source of identity for *Domain* attributes is the specific source system (or system of record). Every attribute within the DWH/BI system can be classified as either *Domain* or *Technical* hence we used "{disjoint, complete}" meta-attributes for specialization relation. We further decided to model domain attributes with two subtypes – fact and dimensional attributes, as they are used in different modes within the dimensional model. Note that the two subtypes have only {*complete*} meta-attribute on their specialization as it is possible for a domain attribute to be included in both the fact table and the dimension table and fulfill different roles in each case.

The technical attributes in a dimension table are used to manage the data and transformation process and are not directly related to business data. Common examples are attributes used for implementation SCD (*start_date*, *end_date*, *is_current*), surrogate keys, audit attributes (*created_by*, *last_modified_on*) or row checksum. These attributes originate exclusively within a DWH/BI environment and are usually generated during transformation of data from source systems.

Domain attributes, on the other hand, are specific for every organization and every DWH/BI solution. Values, data types, and names of these attributes originate from business needs and source systems, and hence are subject to changes derived by evolution of enterprise and its needs.

5.4   Categorization of Fact Attributes

Fact attributes are commonly classified [3,14,19] based on their ability to be aggregated across dimensions. *Additive* attributes can be fully aggregated across all dimensions, making them ideal for operations such as summing sales figures across different regions and times. For example, total sales can be summed across different stores and months. *Non-Additive* attributes cannot be summed across any dimension; an example would be average temperature, where averaging, not summing, makes sense across locations or days. *Semi-Additive* attributes are aggregable across some dimensions but not others; for example, inventory levels can be summed across locations but not time, as you cannot simply add inventory levels from two different months to get a meaningful figure.

In our approach, we decided to model different types of additivity using *Phases* (Fig. 4). The reasoning behind our decision is the following: whether or not a specific attribute can be considered additive is determined by the specific values of that attribute. For example, even though *Revenue* attribute has the potential to be additive, it depends on whether the attribute values are in the same currency. A similar argument could be made for semi-additive attribute – the average of *Temperature* is meaningful only if the ETL system is properly converting values from every source system into a common temperature unit.

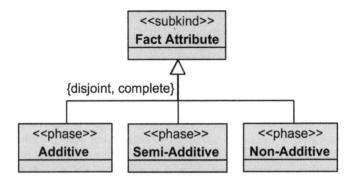

Fig. 4. Categorization of fact attributes based on additivity.

5.5   Categorization of Keys

In this subsection, we present the result of our ontological analysis of different types of database keys.

The root of our classification (depicted in Fig. 5) is an abstract umbrella *Key* which splits keys into two *Subkinds* and two *Phases*.

The *Business Key* (also known as *Natural Key*) is the key from the system of origin. It could be made up of one or several *Domain Attributes*. These attributes directly contribute to the identity of *Business Key*, hence the reason for *essential* stereotype. Specific *Domain attributes* can be parts of multiple *Business Keys*, e.g. attribute *ZIP Code* could be used in tandem with other attributes to create the primary key in the source system.

The *Surrogate Key* is generated within DWH/BI system and it is used for query optimization and resolution of duplicit *Business Keys* occurring when different source systems use the same attributes for *Business Key* or duplication of primary keys during the historization process of data in dimension tables. As with the *Business Key*, the identity of *Surrogate Key* is closely interconnected with the attributes of which the key is made. Unlike the *Business Key*, the

Surrogate Key does not share its attributes with other keys, as it would result in duplicate primary keys in the database.

We also identified two different types of keys based of semantic of their values.

Smart Key is a key with embedded semantics within its value, for example Vehicle Identification Number (VIN), currency/language ISO code or IP address can be all potentially be used as keys and contain additional information as well. *Smart Key*s are usually *Business Key*s, but *Surrogate Key*s can be generated with meaning as well – for example, the primary key of *Holiday* dimension could be a value in format "YYYYMMDD".

The *Simple Key* on the other hand is a meaningless value, examples of this type of keys are GUID or sequential integers generated by the database.

The reason why we decided to model *Smart Key* and *Simple Key* as a *Phase* and not *Subkind* is following – whether or not the key has any semantics is up to the specific value (e.g. "20241332" is not a meaningful value).

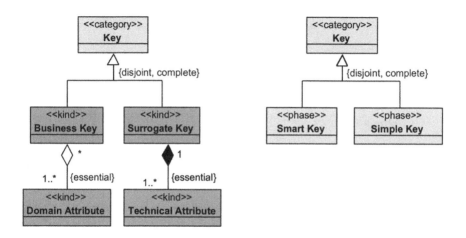

Fig. 5. Categorization of keys.

5.6 Categorization of Dimensions

One way to categorize different types of dimension is on the basis of the concept of conformity (depicted in Fig. 6). The conformity in this context describes whether the concepts modeled and stored in a certain dimension are semantically unified and adhere to the common understanding of that concept throughout the entire business. The dimensions that meet this criterion are said to be *Conformed*.

If only a subset of attributes within the dimension adheres to the conformity criterion, such dimension is with *Limited Conformity*.

The rest of the dimensions are then called *Non-Conformed*.

The concept of conformity is important for drill-across reporting functionality – *Conformed* dimensions ensure consistency in reporting and analysis by providing a uniform view of data across various business areas. For example, a *Client* dimension used in sales, finance, and marketing data marts allows for consistent analysis across these different domains.

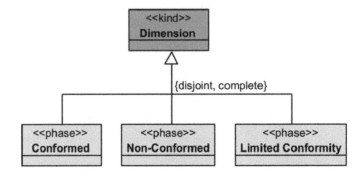

Fig. 6. Categorization of dimensions based on conformity.

5.7   Categorization of Fact Tables

One of the common ways [3,14,19] to categorize fact tables is based on what each business transaction captures in the company and how it will be subsequently used, which in turn affects how transactions of a given type are stored in the database.

Accumulating Snapshot fact tables track the life cycle of a business process, capturing key milestones from start to finish. An example of such process could be the process of shipping item to customer, milestones would in that case represent e.g. order, item dispatch and delivery.

Transactional fact tables record detailed line-level data for each transaction event, e.g. each purchased item.

Periodic Snapshot fact tables aggregate data over a fixed period, such as daily or monthly. These types of tables are used to analyze trends over that time frame. Each type serves distinct analytical needs, from detailed transactional analysis to tracking long-term process performance and trends.

The resulting diagram is depicted in Fig. 7.

5.8   Slowly Changing Dimensions

In Fig. 8 we present the result of the ontological analysis of the relationships between SCDs and attributes and their data change velocity. We decided to model concepts related to historization of attributes in significantly different way than in original model (Fig. 1).

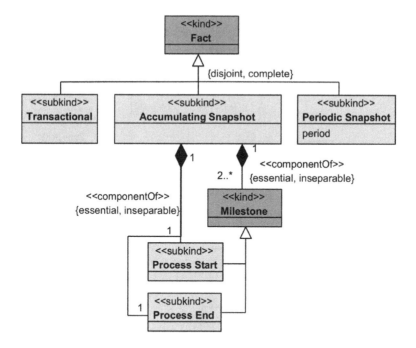

Fig. 7. Categorization of fact tables.

First, we separated four SCDs (0, 1, 2 and 3) into separate concept called *Attribute Historization Policy (AHP)* and its four specializations. This concept is independent of implementation, and it is intended for communication between business stakeholders and developers, as its sole role is to express what kind of historization of data is business interested in. The rest of common SCDs were identified either as combinations of other SCDs or as merely performance optimization of other SCDs or both. The meta-attributes {*essential, inseparable*} indicate that every dimensional attribute must have its *AHP* (*essential*) and that *AHP* can not exist independently of the attribute itself (*inseparable*).

Second, we modeled *AHP* as attribute of every *Dimension Attribute* as it more precisely models the reality – every dimension attribute can be historized independently within every dimension, possibly by combination of several different *AHP*, furthermore concrete implementation (whether baseline or highly optimized) is dictated by expected rate of change of said attribute.

Third, we modeled relationship between *Implementation, AHP* and *Data Change Velocity (DCV)* and *Dimension Attribute*. The concept *DCV* was modeled as *Mode* with three different *Phases*. The motivation for the usage of *Mode* and *Phase* was following - the speed of the change of data can vary over time within each dimension and each attribute, so this property is not rigid and there is no particular speed of data that makes *DCV* switch from one subtype to another.

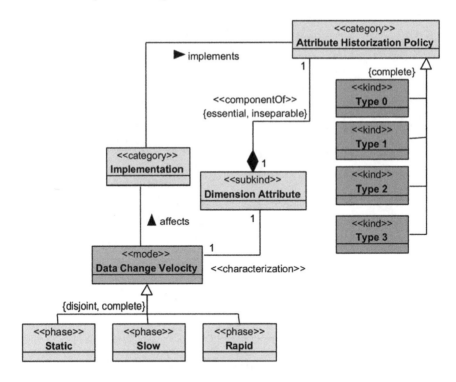

Fig. 8. Relations between types of historization and dimensional attributes.

6   Discussion and Conclusion

In this article we applied formal ontological analysis on several concepts of DWH/BI systems using the OntoUML modeling language. The use of OntoUML concepts helped clarify and expand commonly used concepts within the DWH/BI community and showed potential problems with current naming conventions.

During ontological modeling of SCDs and related concepts, we discovered a semantic misalignment between what SCD represents in minds of developers and business stakeholders. We also consider the concept of SCD to be overloaded from semantic point of view - it encompasses business intent (i.e. to have historical view of data) and implementation details (i.e. how this business need will be implemented in database).

Based on our modeling results and in order to achieve more clearly defined concepts related to SCD functionality, we suggest splitting commonly used terminology of SCDs into business and implementation parts. More specifically, Type 0, 1, 2 and 3 *Attribute Historization Policy* should be used during the collection of business requirements, during dimensional modeling, and during communication between business stakeholders and DWH/BI developers. The concrete implementation of data historization would then be chosen for required business functionality taking into account technological aspects (e.g., volume of data processed) of historization.

This clear conceptual separation of business and implementation realms allows developers to switch and change concrete implementations as needed when data influx into DWH/BI system increases (or decreases) or when better data versioning strategies are discovered without affecting the perceived functionality by end users. Other benefits of this separation is, together with identification of technical and domain attributes, the ability to better and more clearly separate technological aspects of DWH/BI systems into technological layer which could be moved into domain independent templates of code. These templates could then be parameterized using domain-specific requirements – this approach could potentially leverage knowledge from the field of Model-Driven Development. Another application of our suggestion is to hide technological attributes and/or auxiliary tables from the graphical user interface of tools used for development of DWH/BI systems and hence remove unnecessary "technological noise" from the screen.

Based on our current results, we suggest application of our approach on other aspects of BI/DWH, namely – metadata, logical and hardware architecture, specific ETL processes, and reporting, might be beneficial and could yield useful results. In this article we used only concepts from UFO-A ontology, but application of UFO-B on different processes within the DWH/BI environment could potentially yield interesting results as well. For example, modeling the process of inserting new record into dimension table with some type of historization, transformation of ETL scripts implementing certain task from one implementation to another (possibly due to optimization or technological needs), or even transformation of entire architecture from more traditional approach to architecture following the latest trends in the field of DWH.

Application of UFO-C ontology could potentially enhance DWH/BI by offering a structured way to model and analyze organizational behaviors, roles and intentions. It could potentially aid in designing data warehouses that capture and reflect complex social structures and interactions, improving insights into customer behaviors, employee performance and organizational efficiency. By incorporating social and intentional dimensions into BI analyzes, organizations can achieve a deeper understanding of internal and external influences on performance and results, leading potentially to more informed decision-making.

Application of UFO-S in DWH/BI environment could be used to create conceptual models for purposes of service integration between source systems and DWH, description of provided services by DWH to external parties, metadata management and Service License Agreement (SLA) negation. By providing a structured and principled framework for representing services, their properties, and interactions, UFO-S facilitates has the potential to improve integration of heterogeneous data sources, ensuring interoperability and reducing semantic conflicts.

From our experience during our effort so far, we recommend conducting ontological analysis within limited subdomains (e.g., ETL processes) and not the entirety of DWH/BI landscape, as it would be enormous undertaking. The partial results of separate ontological analyses should then be combined into one complex model, which could be further developed into a separate domain ontology for the DWH/BI domain, which would be more suitable for further research.

The main disadvantage of using more expressive modeling language like OntoUML is that the modeler or the reader has to be familiar with its notation or the OntoUML model has to be transformed back to plain UML.

Acknowledgments. This research was supported by the Czech Technical University in Prague grant No. SGS23/206/OHK3/3T/18.

References

1. Devens, R.M.: Cyclopædia of Commercial and Business Anecdotes. D. Appleton and Company, London, New York (1865)
2. Castells, M.: The Information Age: Economy, Society and Culture Volume 1: The Rise of the Network Society, 2nd edn. Wiley Blackwell, Oxford (2010)
3. Sherman, R.: Business Intelligence Guidebook: From Data Integration to Analytics. Elsevier, Morgan Kaufmann is an Imprint of Elsevier, Amsterdam (2015)
4. Khan, S., Qader, M.R., Thirunavukkarasu, K., Abimannan, S.: Analysis of business intelligence impact on organizational performance. In: 2020 International Conference on Data Analytics for Business and Industry: Way Towards a Sustainable Economy (ICDABI). Presented at the 2020 International Conference on Data Analytics for Business and Industry: Way Towards a Sustainable Economy (ICDABI). IEEE, Sakheer, Bahrain, pp. 1–4 (2020). https://doi.org/10.1109/ICDABI51230.2020.9325610
5. Martins, A., Martins, P., Caldeira, F., Sá, F.: An evaluation of how big-data and data warehouses improve business intelligence decision making. In: Rocha, Á., Adeli, H., Reis, L.P., Costanzo, S., Orovic, I., Moreira, F. (eds.) Trends and Innovations in Information Systems and Technologies, vol. 1, pp. 609–619. Springer, Cham (2020). https://doi.org/10.1007/978-3-030-45688-7_61
6. Guizzardi, G., Benevides, A., Fonseca, C., Porello, D., Almeida, J., Prince Sales, T.: UFO: Unified foundational ontology. Appl. Ontol. (2021). https://doi.org/10.3233/AO-210256
7. Studer, R., Benjamins, V.R., Fensel, D.: Knowledge engineering: principles and methods. Data Knowl. Eng. **25**, 161–197 (1998). https://doi.org/10.1016/S0169-023X(97)00056-6
8. Nardi, J.C., et al.: Towards a commitment-based reference ontology for services, pp. 175–184. IEEE (2013). https://doi.org/10.1109/EDOC.2013.28
9. Husserl, E., Moran, D.: Logical Investigations, International Library of Philosophy. Routledge, London, New York (2001)
10. Inmon, W.H.: Building the Data Warehouse, 4th edn. Wiley, Indianapolis (2005)
11. Inmon, W.H., Strauss, D., Neushloss, G.: DW 2.0: The Architecture for the Next Generation of Data Warehousing. Morgan Kaufmann, Amsterdam, Boston (2008)
12. Kimball, R., Caserta, J.: The Data Warehouse ETL Toolkit: Practical Techniques for Extracting, Cleaning, Conforming, and Delivering Data. Wiley, Indianapolis (2004)

13. Linstedt, D., Olschimke, M.: Building a Scalable Data Warehouse with Data Vault 2.0. Morgan Kaufmann, An Imprint of Elsevier, Amsterdam, Boston, Heidelberg (2015)
14. Corr, L., Stagnitto, J.: Agile Data Warehouse Design: Collaborative Dimensional Modeling, from Whiteboard to Star Schema, revised edn. Decision Press, Leeds (2014)
15. Guizzardi, G., Baião, F., Lopes, M., Falbo, R.: The role of foundational ontologies for domain ontology engineering: an industrial case study in the domain of oil and gas exploration and production. Int. J. Inf. Syst. Model. Des. (IJISMD) **1**, 1–22 (2010)
16. Griffo, C., Almeida, J.P.A., Guizzardi, G.: A pattern for the representation of legal relations in a legal core ontology. Front. Artif. Intell. Appl. **294**, 191–194 (2016). https://doi.org/10.3233/978-1-61499-726-9-191
17. Dhaouadi, A., Bousselmi, K., Gammoudi, M.M., Monnet, S., Hammoudi, S.: Data warehousing process modeling from classical approaches to new trends: main features and comparisons. Data **7**, 113 (2022). https://doi.org/10.3390/data7080113
18. Yessad, L., Labiod, A.: Comparative study of data warehouses modeling approaches: Inmon, Kimball and Data Vault. In: 2016 International Conference on System Reliability and Science (ICSRS). Presented at the 2016 International Conference on System Reliability and Science (ICSRS), pp. 95–99. IEEE, Paris, France (2016). https://doi.org/10.1109/ICSRS.2016.7815845
19. Kimball, R., Ross, M.: The Data Warehouse Toolkit: The Definitive Guide to Dimensional Modeling, 3rd edn. Wiley, Indianapolis (2013)

Quality Evaluation of a DSML Supporting Model-Driven IoT Development for Air Conditioning Facilities

Benjamin Nast[1]([✉])[iD] and Kurt Sandkuhl[1,2][iD]

[1] Rostock University, 18051 Rostock, Germany
{benjamin.nast,kurt.sandkuhl}@uni-rostock.de
[2] Jönköping University, 55111 Jönköping, Sweden

Abstract. Model-Driven Development (MDD) is considered an effective technique for Internet of Things (IoT) application development. Our observation is that existing model-based approaches for IoT solutions focus on the software and systems perspective and show a need for more integration with organizational and business model aspects. Therefore, we developed a method and tool support for developing IoT applications in the field of air conditioning facilities. In this work, we applied quality criteria to evaluate the included Domain-Specific Modeling Language (DSML). To practically validate the modeling language as such and also the way it can be used and supported by the tool, we performed a real-world use case. The main contributions of this paper are a quality evaluation of the DSML and the tool support and lessons learned from both.

Keywords: Domain-Specific Modeling Language · Modeling Method · Model-Driven Development · Internet of Things · Notation Evaluation · Quality Evaluation · SEQUAL · MIoTA

1 Introduction

Model-Driven Development (MDD) is considered an effective technique for Internet of Things (IoT) application development [4,21]. Code generated automatically due to model transformations increases productivity and supports consistency through automation [3]. The complexity of IoT application development, as well as efficient and (partially) automated implementation, can be addressed by meta-models for domain-specific applications. MDD can be enabled by defining a Domain-Specific Modeling Language (DSML) to describe system requirements [6]. These are easier to specify, maintain, and understand. The integrity of a model can be preserved by defined semantics or syntax. They also prevent nonsensical models. Specific graphical notations often provide a concrete syntax that improves the models' understanding and clarity.

Our previous work [14] identified the need for a DSML in the area of IoT application development by analyzing business requirements and existing literature. We also performed a systematic literature review, which shows there is

M. Malinova Mandelburger et al. (Eds.): EDEWC 2023, LNBIP 510, pp. 52–72, 2024.
https://doi.org/10.1007/978-3-031-58935-5_4

no validated approach that combines technological and organizational aspects in all phases of the development process, and there is no specific support for Small and Medium-Sized Enterprises (SMEs) [15].

In this paper, we perform a quality evaluation of a DSML that supports model-driven IoT application development for air conditioning facilities. It is included in a modeling tool that does not require any special IT skills at the application level and thus allows configuration by a domain expert. The DSML was developed in an industrial use case, and our goal was to optimize energy consumption and create a basis for predictive maintenance. This is realized by equipping facilities with as few sensors as possible. As a result, an IoT-based system creates the basis for these, but also for new business services.

The paper is structured as follows: Sect. 2 introduces the topic of quality evaluation in conceptual modeling. Our DSML and tool support are described in Sect. 3. The evaluation approach is described in Sect. 4. In Sect. 5, we discuss the evaluation of the notation, followed by the practical evaluation of the DSML and the tool support in Sect. 6. Lastly, Sect. 7 outlines the limitations of our work, summarizes our findings, and provides an outlook on future work.

2 Quality Evaluation in Conceptual Modeling

Accurate representations are crucial to understanding highly complex problem domains that exist in today's organizations. Conceptual modeling creates representations and abstractions that remove much of the complexity found in real-world problem domains [17]. A conceptual modeling method consists of a modeling language, modeling procedure, and mechanisms and algorithms [7]. The modeling language is described by its syntax, semantics, and notation. It contains the elements that can be used to describe a model. The modeling procedure describes the steps for applying the modeling language to create models.

Many general-purpose modeling languages, like Unified Modeling Language (UML) and Business Process Model and Notation (BPMN), have been designed. Currently, there is a growing emphasis on developing DSMLs [2] that are customized to the needs of a particular application domain and its stakeholders. The modeling language to be evaluated in this work belongs to this. It is part of a modeling method that conforms to the definition given above.

Quality evaluation in conceptual modeling can, in general, be performed with a focus on different perspectives of "quality", such as the quality of the modeling process [10], the quality of the modeling result [22], the quality levels of conceptual modeling [17], or the quality of modeling methods [20]. From the perspective of our research work, the model as such and its usage are in focus, which motivates the selection of a quality framework that integrates various quality aspects with emphasis on the modeling result.

We selected the Semiotic Model Quality Framework (SEQUAL) [9] as it has three properties relevant to our research: (1) SEQUAL provides the possibility to distinguish between quality characteristics and means to achieve these characteristics (goals). This allows us to consider the requirements of the model from the field of air conditioning facilities and how they were implemented. (2) SEQUAL addresses quality on various semiotic levels, such as syntax, semantics, and pragmatics. It is important to include the modeling language as such and also how it is used in the case study and supported by the tool. (3) Furthermore, SEQUAL acknowledges that models often are created in collaboration between those involved in modeling, whose knowledge of the modeling domain changes as modeling takes place. IoT development in the field of air conditioning facilities, to our experience, involves different stakeholders in such a collaboration process.

SEQUAL proposes to distinguish between different aspects of model quality:

- **Physical Quality** addresses the fact that the way the model is presented (i.e., its externalization) is accessible to the users of the model.
- **Syntactic Quality** refers to the coherence between a model and the modeling language that is used for modeling. This could be evaluated by comparing the model and its meta-model.
- **Semantic Quality** refers to the correspondence between a model (or its meta-model) and the modeling domain. The meaning of the concepts in a domain has to be equivalent to the corresponding concepts in the model.
  Closely related is **Perceived Semantic Quality**, which addresses the question of whether actors from the domain think that the meaning of concepts in the model fits the meaning of the same concepts in the domain. It serves as an operational surrogate for Semantic Quality because it does not require verifying correspondence between the model and the domain but rather between the user's interpretation of the model and the domain knowledge.
- **Empirical Quality** and **Pragmatic Quality** are tightly coupled with the view of the model users, which in SEQUAL are described as social actors.
  Empirical Quality compares different models created by a modeler to express the same understanding but implemented differently (e.g., one model shows line crossings, and another model is designed to avoid line crossings).
  Social Pragmatic Quality refers to how well the model is understood by human actors, comparing the modeler's intended understanding of the model with the model user's actual understanding.
  Technical Pragmatic Quality defines to what extent tools can interpret the model.
- **Social Quality** addresses the question of whether actors agree on the interpretation of the model.
- **Deontic Quality** investigates if all elements of a model contribute to fulfilling the goals of modeling and if all goals of modeling are addressed through the model.

3   Modeling Language and Tool Support

This section introduces our DSML and its tool support, along with the use case that informed their development. A more detailed description of the whole modeling method, which is named MIoTA (Modeling IoT Applications for Air

Conditioning Facilities)[1], can be found in [16]. We used the meta-modeling platform ADOxx[2] for the implementation [18]. It is a platform for the development and implementation of modeling methods. Using ADOxx allows us to realize full-fledged modeling software that contains procedures and functionalities in the form of mechanisms and algorithms in addition to the modeling language.

3.1   Use Case and Requirements

The modeling language and tool support were created in an industrial use case in collaboration with an SME that builds, operates, and maintains air conditioning facilities. The aim was to enhance energy efficiency by equipping facilities with as few sensors as possible. Low-cost technologies can save up to 30% of energy in most facilities by identifying faults [8,12].

Numerous components must collaborate seamlessly for industrial air conditioning facilities to function effectively. Monitoring their internal operations requires a variety of sensors. However, interpreting the signal from these sensors is complex and requires significant pre-processing of the data to be of value.

With the increasing automation of control technology, data volume is growing rapidly. Intelligent data processing for direct and indirect processes is necessary to operate energy-efficient facilities. Therefore, there is a considerable need for system solutions that enable self-recognition, self-organized learning, and system control. This results in an IoT-based system that not only establishes the foundation for this but also enables new business services.

The intended IoT solution aims to offer diagnostic support for improving both the air conditioning facility and operating procedures of the enterprise under review in the case study. It must process vast amounts of data from diverse sources. Furthermore, it should integrate smoothly into the daily operations of the case study company and facilitate the provision of new business services.

In [15], we derived requirements for the overall system in collaboration with employees of the use case company. Frequent inspections of facilities in operation uncover deviations from established energy efficiency but only identify faults present during the inspection. The system must provide maintenance support, identify malfunctions and operational errors, enable predictive maintenance, and facilitate energetic inspections. In Germany, these inspections are legally required procedures to evaluate the energy efficiency of industrial-sized air conditioning facilities.

The tool support should have a familiar user interface (req. 1) and the capability to graphically illustrate facilities (req. 2) to assist technicians in the development of IoT solutions and when presenting information to clients regarding various matters such as upgrades, maintenance, or replacements. A DSML with an employee-friendly notation should be utilized to achieve this objective.

To realize significant energy savings through facility comparisons of similar configurations (and to account for heterogeneity), essential data must be

---

[1] https://www.omilab.org/MIoTA/.
[2] https://www.adoxx.org/.

collected from each facility. This configuration data incorporates operator, component, and sensor information, among other items. A data type, value range, and matching unit are specified, and default values may be included for meaningful data analysis when data is missing. The configuration data was compiled by experts in a way that allows the deduction of the necessary sensors required for each facility. It allows the calculation of many other data points in a facility (e.g., calculation of transported air based on the measured pressure difference of the fans in conjunction with the performance data from the manual), so we need a minimum number of sensors. Combining this data with corresponding sensor data enables the derivation of relevant energy-saving measures. For instance, it is now possible to determine if a fan is operating at its best performance or if rooms or areas of a building are being air-conditioned unnecessarily. The tool should be able to collect (req. 3) and export (req. 4) this data and assign unique IDs to the facilities, components, and sensors (req. 5).

3.2   Modeling Language

The DSML was developed to model air conditioning facilities and their components. Its visual notation is based on the European standard DIN EN 12792 and the knowledge of domain experts involved in our project. The current version is the result of an iterative and incremental development process (see [16]), which we consider suitable for the development task and essential for achieving a model that fulfills the requirements of the application domain. The results of the work described in this paper will lead to the third major version, all of which were validated with the end users and grounded in requirements.

There are different elements for the components of a facility, the type of air, and different sensor types. Additionally, there is an item for configuration data storage and notes. As they are not a part of the actual modeling of a facility, they are the only ones in color. The DSML contains one relation type for the logical connection of components and air types, which also shows the airflow direction in the model. Figure 1 shows the visual notation.

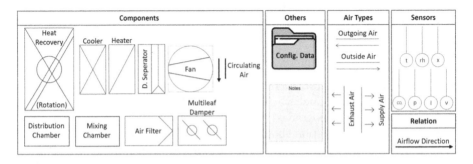

Fig. 1. Visual Notation of the DSML.

The components are, e.g., Fan, Cooler, and Heat Recovery, and can each have incoming and outgoing relations. Some of them have several visual representations, depending on the specific type of component. The types of air are Outgoing, Outside, Exhaust, and Supply Air. They each have only one incoming or outgoing relation. A sensor is represented with a circle and a line to the component or place in the model. The specific type is represented with letters in the circle (e.g., Temperature (t), Relative Humidity (rh), or CO_2 Content (CO_2)). In the object Configuration Data, information about the facility, its components, and sensors are saved as attribute values. In addition to these elements, we have objects for grouping components (e.g., in Active/Passive Area or Room), an object to add photos in the model (e.g., to use them as background or add several views of a facility), and an object for Notes, which can also be shown on the modeling surface. It is possible to rotate the orientation of the modeling objects and also to change the size. Figure 2 shows a model example of an existing facility.

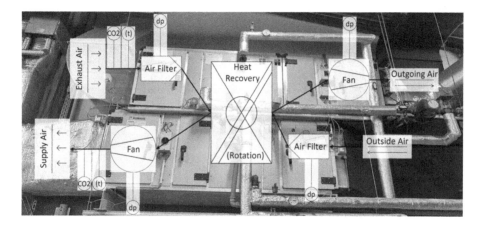

Fig. 2. Example of a Model of an Air Conditioning Facility.

The model contains two Air Filters, two Fans, a Heat Recovery (type: Rotation), and the elements for the Supply, Exhaust, Outgoing, and Outside Air. The Fans and the Filters are equipped with a sensor for measuring the pressure difference. The Exhaust and Supply Air are equipped with CO_2 Content and Temperature sensors. This section demonstrates the provision of a familiar user interface (req. 1) and the capability to graphically represent facilities (req. 2).

3.3   Tool Functions

The developed tool not only includes the DSML for air conditioning facilities. It provides several functionalities to support the technician in modeling and configuring the IoT application. The creation of a model in the tool starts with

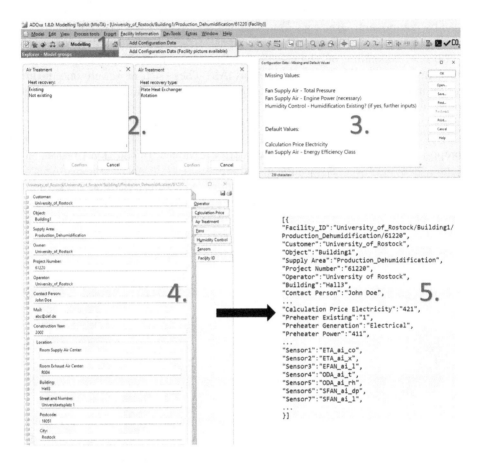

Fig. 3. Process of Entering the Configuration Data in the MIoTA Tool.

the input of configuration data (req. 3). Figure 3 shows the process in the tool with the associated steps. The input can be started from a menu item (**step 1**). Dialog boxes are used to speed up the input (**step 2**), and corresponding queries are only made if the respective components are included in the facility. Value ranges have been defined to avoid errors during inputs. If values are entered outside these ranges, an error message appears, and a valid value must be entered. For some attributes, default values are displayed in the dialog boxes to further speed up input. These values are fictitious and necessary for meaningful data analysis and are used when real data is missing (e.g., the price of electricity for a customer).

The modeling elements are created automatically during the input of the configuration data if they exist in the respective facility. Based on the configuration data, we differentiate the facilities into two different groups. For the two groups, we have a given set of sensors, which must be installed and are also automatically added to the model. We consider facilities with Heating or Cooling or both, and the second group additionally has Humidification or Dehumidification, or both. Sensors for measuring CO_2 Content are optional for both groups.

After entering the configuration data, completeness is confirmed, or a list of missing values is output (**step 3**). It also indicates whether the missing values are necessary and which entries have been set as default values. The list can be customized, exported, or printed.

In the next step, the user can adjust the modeling elements by correctly arranging and connecting the components or adding or removing them. To change the configuration data or add missing values, the notebook can be opened (**step 4**). It is divided into different chapters of the configuration data and stores the entered information. Furthermore, the identifiers for the sensors and the Facility_ID are shown. The configuration data can be represented as a JSON file (**step 5**).

Figure 4 shows the further functionalities of the MIoTA tool. **Step 6** includes three menu icons:

- **Execute AdoScript:** Enables the execution and testing of AdoScript code in the modeling tool.
- **Check Sensors and Configuration Data:** This icon is used to check if a sensor appears more than once in a model. It also verifies the configuration data (refer to step 3).
- **Add CO_2 Content Sensors:** Automatically adds CO_2 content sensors with a specific designation if they are not already included in the model.

Fig. 4. MIoTA Tool Functionalities.

After the model and the data are adjusted, the information can be sent as a JSON file via an HTTP request to an Application Programming Interface (API) in the cloud in **step 7** (req. 4). The endpoint can be configured by selecting "Change URL". Before sending the data, the tool again checks the data (e.g., value ranges, plausibility), if duplicate sensors are created, and if all necessary data is entered.

The data is stored in a document-centric database located in the cloud and is then used for the (partly automatic) cloud service configuration and subsequent data analysis. The uploaded data also enables the physical configuration of the sensors, and it shows which types are needed and where they need to be installed in the facility. For presentations or internal purposes, it is also possible to export a documentation of the model.

The developed meta-model (see [16]) allows the unique identification of the modeling elements. This is necessary to support the automatic cloud configuration and further data analyses. Each facility, component, and sensor is assigned a unique identifier (req. 5). The facility ID and sensor ID are used together to name the Message Queuing Telemetry Transport (MQTT) topics, which informs the cloud broker where to expect new data.

4   Evaluation Approach

As a general framework for quality evaluation of the DSML presented in Sect. 3 we use SEQUAL. Based on the introduction to SEQUAL in Sect. 2, this section explains how the different SEQUAL aspects are investigated and the results obtained. For some aspects, the evaluation has already been performed in previous work. Table 1 summarizes the evaluation approach and results.

Table 1. SEQUAL-based Evaluation Approach.

Quality Aspect	Evaluation Approach	Evaluation Result
Physical	Moody's "Physics of Notations" & expert interview	Coherence confirmed in Sects. 5 and 6
Syntactic	Coherence of meta-model of the DSML and its implementation in the modeling tool	Coherence was confirmed in [14]
Semantic	Coherence of concept of meaning in domain and concept in meta-model	Coherence was confirmed in [14]
Perceived Semantic	Expert interview: Is the meaning in the domain consistent with the meaning in the model?	Coherence confirmed in Sect. 6
Empirical	Usage of models in case study and observation of different actors regarding model understanding	So far only partially evaluation confirming that actors comprehend the model in Sect. 6
Technical Pragmatic	Machine-readability of meta-model by tool	Given by the implementation in the meta-modeling tool
Social (Pragmatic)	Usage of models in case study and observation of different actors regarding model understanding	So far only partially evaluation confirming that actors comprehend the model in Sect. 6
Deontic	Design of DSML based on requirements followed by evaluation for target groups & expert interview	Coherence was confirmed in [14] and Sect. 6

The Physical Quality was evaluated by applying the criteria from Moody's "Physics of Notations" [13] (Sect. 5) and through questions in an expert interview with users of the DSML based on these (Sect. 6). It has been confirmed that the modelers are able to express their intended understanding through the externalization of the model. This ensures that the externalized model is available to the relevant social and technical actors. The meta-model and tool support guarantee that the model is consistent, up-to-date, and aligned with the modeling goals. Only authorized individuals have access to view or modify the model, ensuring security.

Coherence with Syntactic and Semantic Quality was confirmed in our previous work [14]. To achieve this goal, we evaluated the coherence of the DSML and its implementation in the modeling tool and the coherence of the concept of meaning in the domain and the concept in the meta-model in collaboration with domain experts.

The evaluation of the Perceived Semantic Quality was also part of the expert interview (Sect. 6), in which we checked whether the meaning in the domain matched that in the model. The focus was on the criteria of correctness, relevancy, completeness, consistency, and realism. This demonstrated that the objectives of perceived validity and completeness were achieved.

Technical Pragmatic Quality was considered by assessing the machine-readability of the meta-model by the tool, which is given due to the implementation in the meta-modeling tool.

To ensure coherence with the Deontic Quality, we started by collecting requirements for designing the DSML through interviews with domain experts [14]. The expert interview in Sect. 6 serves to re-evaluate the implementation of requirements after various modifications have been made in the previous versions. It has been confirmed that all statements in the model contribute to fulfilling the modeling goals and that the model addresses all of the goals of modeling.

The evaluation of Empirical, Social, and Social Pragmatic Quality has only been partial so far. To assess these aspects, we used models in the case study and observed the different actors regarding the model understanding (Sect. 6). It was confirmed that social actors (modelers) understand the model by comparing the modeler's intended understanding of the model with the model user's actual understanding (Social Pragmatic Quality). In the future, it is also necessary to compare different models created by different social actors (modelers) to express the same understanding but implemented differently (e.g., one model shows line crossings, while another avoids line crossing) to completely assess the coherence with the Empirical and Socical Quality. To further assess the Social Pragmatic Quality, the understanding of users who were not involved in the modeling process should be compared with the modeler's intended understanding of the model.

5   Evaluation of the Notation

As mentioned before, we applied the criteria of Moody's "Physics of Notations" [13] as part of the assessment of the Physical Quality of our modeling language. This is an important work on the quality of visual notations and mainly focuses on comprehensibility. A language involves more than its visual notation. Distinctions can be made between the symbols and the concepts behind them, as well as the abstract syntax for these concepts [7]. SEQUAL is a more comprehensive approach to language quality that integrates Moody's work.

5.1 Criteria for Evaluation

There are nine principles for the design of cognitively effective visual notations defined by Moody [13]. The following is a brief presentation of these principles.

- **Semiotic Clarity:** A one-to-one correspondence between symbols and concepts of the notation is required by this principle. There are four different possible deficiencies of visual notations defined with respect to Semiotic Clarity: (1) Symbol Redundancy, if multiple symbols represent the same concept; (2) Symbol Overload, if a symbol represents multiple concepts; (3) Symbol Excess, if there are symbols that do not correspond to a concept of the notation, and (4) Symbol Deficit, if there are notation concepts without a corresponding symbol.
- **Perceptual Discriminability:** The idea behind this principle is that symbols must be clearly distinguishable from each other. A number of suggestions are represented to reach this goal, assuring Visual Distance of symbols by using a high number of visual variables (e.g., color, size, shape) to make them visually different. The most important visual variable is shape, and this is called Primacy of Shape. Additional recommendations include using text to differentiate between symbols (Textual Differentiation), using unique values for at least one visual variable (Perceptual Popout), and using more than one visual variable in order to make a difference between symbols (Redundant Coding).
- **Semantic Transparency:** This principle describes the extent to which the meaning of a symbol can be derived from its appearance. This can range from semantically immediate symbols, where the meaning can be inferred without additional information, over semantically opaque symbols, where there is no link between appearance and meaning, to semantically perverse symbols, which imply a wrong meaning for the model user. A notation's performance with respect to this principle depends on the model users and should be evaluated in experiments. Moody's general recommendations for that are the use of symbols that represent real objects (Perceptual Resemblance) and special graphical relations (Semantically Transparent Relations) such as intersections or trees. It is possible to check whether these recommendations are implemented in a notation.
- **Complexity Management:** According to this principle, explicit mechanisms are required to deal with complexity. The number of elements used is a simple measure of the complexity of a model. Limitations of perception and cognition are reached with increasing model size, and the comprehensibility of the models suffers. Notations should, therefore, provide mechanisms for reducing complexity. Modularization and Hierarchy (Levels of Abstraction) are the main mechanisms to reach this goal.

- **Cognitive Integration:** A mechanism to integrate information from different models is, for example, Conceptual Integration. An overview of the model and sub-models is given by providing concepts on a high abstraction level that can be combined in order to relate the used sub-models. To support the model user with navigation in the model space, there is Perceptual Integration.
- **Visual Expressiveness:** While the Visual Distance (see above) considers the pairwise difference of concepts with regard to visual variables, this principle addresses the use of visual variables throughout the whole graphical notation. So the question is, what number of visual variables is used to express semantics and to distinguish between concepts (Information-carrying Variables), and which number of visual variables is not formally used (Free Variables)? A total of eight variables are defined by Moody: Horizontal Position, Vertical Position, Size, Brightness, Color, Texture, Shape, and Orientation. It is recommended to use as many Information-carrying variables as possible. So there is a maximum of eight.
- **Dual Coding:** In general, text is not a good way to create visual notation. However, it is useful to support visual notations with text. This can be done by Annotations or Hybrid Symbols, which combine text and graphical objects.
- **Graphic Economy:** This principle addresses the number of available symbols for modeling. A maximum of six symbols is recommended. Having an overabundance of symbols makes it difficult for the modeler to be clear about which symbols can be used. Moody proposes three strategies to increase Graphic Economy: (1) Reduce Semantic Complexity to reduce the number of concepts used, (2) Introduce Symbol Deficit, and (3) Increase Visual Expressiveness.
- **Cognitive Fit:** Different visual dialects are proposed here for different tasks and target groups. It is assumed that problem-solving performance is influenced by problem representation, task characteristics, and problem-solver skills. A problem representation should, therefore, fit the two other factors.
- **Interactions among Principles:** Between the described principles for the design of the notation, there are also interdependencies. Knowing the interactions allows to synergize (principles support each other) or compromise (principles conflict with one another). The introduction of a Symbol Deficit, for example, and thus the reduction of Semiotic Clarity, promotes Graphic Economy. Another example is that the greater the number of symbols (Graphic Economy), the more difficult it is to distinguish between them (Perceptual Discriminability).

5.2   Application of the Criteria

The evaluation of the notation was performed in two phases by the authors and two independent researchers. After a brief discussion of Moody's principles between the researchers, a joint understanding was confirmed. The first phase was that everyone evaluated the notation independently of each other and documented their individual results. In the second phase, the results were compared and integrated. The comparison showed no significant differences between the researchers.

Table 2. Application of Moody's Criteria.

Moody's Principles	Application of the Principles
1: Semiotic Clarity	Fulfilled: No redundant symbols, no symbol overload, no superfluous symbols, no missing symbols
2: Perceptual Discriminabilty	Partly implemented: Different shapes with the exception of sensor symbol
3: Semantic Transparency	Fulfilled: Symbols correspond to standard in the domain
4: Complexity Management	Not implemented: No levels of abstraction included so far
5: Cognitive Integration	Not implemented: Integration of different models not applicable; no sub-models used
6: Visual Expressiveness	Fulfilled: Pairwise comparison of symbols confirms that principle is met
7: Dual Coding	Fulfilled: All symbols have corresponding text
8: Graphic Economy	Partly implemented: More than six symbols are used; separate symbol set for target groups?
9: Cognitive Fit	Not implemented so far; future work

The final result is summarized in Table 2. It shows for each principle if it has been fully implemented ("Fulfilled"), implemented to some extent ("Partly implemented"), or not been implemented ("Not implemented"). The following is a description of the results and (possible) interactions with other principles. Semiotic Clarity, Semantic Transparency, Visual Expressiveness, and Dual Coding have been fulfilled.

– **Semiotic Clarity:** A one-to-one correspondence between symbols and concepts of the notation is given. There are no multiple symbols representing the same concept (Symbol Redundancy), no symbols representing multiple concepts (Symbol Overload), no symbols that do not correspond to a concept of the notation (Symbol Excess), and no concepts without a corresponding symbol (Symbol Deficit). It should be noted here that the two researchers who are not involved in the project were unable to provide meaningful answers to Symbol Excess and Symbol Deficit due to a lack of domain knowledge.
– **Semantic Transparency:** According to this principle, the performance of a notation depends on the model users. Since the intended users are familiar with the standard, the Semantic Transparency is fulfilled. The two researchers involved in the project (and also the results in Sect. 6.3) confirm this. It is

unlikely that a novice would be able to guess the meaning of any of the symbols.

- **Visual Expressiveness:** The notation uses five visual variables (Shape, Color, Orientation, Size, and Brightness), resulting in a Visual Expressiveness of five. Color is really helpful here for separating the additional elements (Configuration Data and Notes) from the actual notation for air conditioning facilities. Orientation is enabled for each element (except Configuration Data and Notes) and is dependent on the airflow direction. There are possibilities for improvement because the range of Shapes is limited, and most of them are abstract geometrical shapes. Brightness only uses two different levels (dotted and solid lines), and regarding Size, only a thick line is used for the relation (Airflow Direction).
- **Dual Coding:** All symbols of the notation have corresponding text. For Sensor and Chamber symbols, the text is necessary to distinguish. For the other symbols, it isn't necessary for the domain experts (model users) but important for customers who will also see the model.

More important are the principles that have not been implemented or were only partly implemented, as they indicate improvement potential. Perceptual Discriminability and Graphic Economy have been partly fulfilled.

- **Perceptual Discriminability:** Perceptual Discriminability has only been partly fulfilled because the sensor symbols (circle with a line attached) all look similar, as the type of sensor is only indicated by the text in the circle. One way to improve Perceptual Discriminability is to remove the line from the symbol and instead use a relation from the component equipped with the sensor to the actual sensor. This would not only improve the discriminability but also the expressiveness of the actual model because the relation between component and sensor is made explicit instead of implicitly representing it by positioning component and sensor side by side. The disadvantage of separating circle and line is that the resulting new sensor symbol (circle with text) no longer complies with the sensor symbol established in the application domain (circle with line). However, as the connecting line is still displayed as a visualization of the relation, this change seems tolerable.
- **Graphic Economy:** Moody's principle of Graphic Economy recommends using no more than six symbols. The DSML does not follow this recommendation as we decided to follow the stakeholder requirement to implement the symbol set used in the application domain, which has more than six symbols. One way to improve the tool in this respect would be to distinguish between different user groups of the DSML (Cognitive Fit) and tailor the symbol sets available to each group accordingly. However, this would still result in more than six symbols for each group. In our case, assessing the cognitive manageability of the number of graphic symbols is different because the language users familiar with the symbols.

Complexity Management, Cognitive Integration, and Cognitive Fit have not been implemented so far.

- **Complexity Management:** Different levels of abstraction (e.g., sub-models) are a possible way to implement the principle of Complexity Management. So far, the DSML does not include different levels, as the domain experts prefer to visualize all components in a model permanently. However, "grouping" components according to their location (e.g., using the Room class) by introducing transparent containers (rectangular boxes) is a starting point to manage complexity without losing transparency. In the future, it is possible that various model types will be available based on the type of facility. Each model will only include the necessary components and sensors to reduce complexity. In our case, this principle does not appear to be too relevant, as the modeling objects are mostly created automatically based on the configuration data entered.
- **Cognitive Integration:** The integration of different models is not applicable in our case because we are currently not using sub-models. However, this can become relevant in the future (see Complexity Management).
- **Cognitive Fit:** Currently, the notation consists of a single visual dialect used for all purposes, so it does not support Cognitive Fit. This can also become relevant in the future when we will distinguish between different user groups.

This section conducted a systematic analysis of our notation based on a set of empirically and theoretically grounded principles for the design of visual notations. The analysis has revealed several issues that may hinder usability and effectiveness in practice. Based on this, we have derived recommendations for improvement and to remove potential barriers to its adoption in practice. However, some points cannot be realized or are not considered useful in our case due to domain-specific requirements.

6 Evaluation of the Language and Tool Support in Use

To practically evaluate the DSML and the tool support, we conducted a modeling session based on the Thinking Aloud Method [1] followed by a guided expert interview. The following is a description of the setting of the modeling session, how we derived our research questions (RQs) and questions for the interview, and the results.

6.1 Modeling Session

The session was conducted with two employees of the case study company who will use the tool in the future. The employees were trained in the tool before but had no further experience in modeling. Requirements for the tool were closely coordinated with them during development.

In the session, we sat together in a room, and a model of a real facility was created. One employee took the lead in modeling, and the other assisted. The model creation took about 50 min. During the session, the employees were asked to think out loud and discuss the inputs.

During the session, notes were written about the spoken thoughts, and also some requests were made. The necessary documents and data for the model creation were collected in advance. Therefore, the session's time refers only to the creation of the model. In practice, gathering all the information about a facility takes longer. In this way, however, we can measure the time required, which relates exclusively to the use of the tool.

6.2   Interview and Research Questions

The evaluation of the usability of the tool is primarily based on a guided interview with the employees. According to Döring and Bortz [5], guided interviews can provide promising information for unexplored and unpredictable outcomes. They also defined guidelines to execute them properly: a) contextual preparation by determining the topic, the RQs, the target group (i.e., participants and interviewers), and the interview technique; b) defining the questions for the guided interview; and c) practicing the interview in advance. Participants' perceptions of the modeling session conducted in advance were explored and addressed as part of our interview. Based on the impressions of the participants, we investigated if 1) the modeling session was conducted properly, 2) the graphical notation has a good Physical Quality, 3) the process of creating a model is good, 4) the tool makes a good impression, and 5) the Perceived Semantic Quality is given.

The participants' answers are based on their experiences with the tool so far but mainly on the performed modeling session. Therefore, we challenged our approach with the following interview questions, which help answer the RQs:

RQ 1: Was the modeling session conducted well?

1.1 : Was the duration appropriate?
1.2 : How was it thinking out loud while modeling?
1.3 : How was it directly answering questions while modeling?

To practically evaluate the Physical Quality of the graphical notation, we based our RQs on the design principles for good notations by Moody [13] (see Sect. 3.2). As mentioned in Sect. 3.3, there are no levels of abstraction included (Complexity Management), there is no integration of different models because no sub-models are used (Cognitive Integration), and there are no different dialects for different tasks or user groups (Cognitive Fit). Thus, those principles are not meaningfully evaluable with our case study, and there are no questions about them:

RQ 2: How is the Physical Quality of the graphical notation?

2.1 : How easy is the distinction of the objects?
2.2 : Is the number of different visualizations appropriate?
2.3 : Are the elements intuitive and understandable?
2.4 : Is the use of text appropriate?
   The following RQ was defined to evaluate how the process of creating a model is perceived and how the tool supports it:

RQ 3: Are the process and tool support for creating a model good?

3.1 : Is it easy to place the elements in the right place?
3.2 : Is it easy not to forget something?
3.3 : How useful are the supportive functions?
3.4 : What is the ratio of benefit and effort?

Then, we asked whether the tool is an appealing base platform for modeling air conditioning facilities: As our tool is based on the ADOxx meta-modeling platform, we started with questions about the given surface, menu items, and icons. Further, we asked how easy it will be to integrate the tool into daily business, whether the tool will be used in the future, and how:

RQ 4: How good is the overall impression of the tool?

4.1 : How is the surface perceived?
4.2 : How clear are the menu items and icons?
4.3 : How easy is the integration of the tool in daily business?
4.4 : How will the tool be used in the future?

Finally, we asked questions about the created model to check to what extent the Perceived Semantic Quality could be realized. We used the work of Maes and Poels [11] as a guide to form these questions. In [19], the authors derived different criteria relevant to the Perceived Semantic Quality to which the questions can be assigned: correctness (questions 5.1), relevancy (question 5.2), completeness (question 5.3), consistency (question 5.4), and realism (question 5.5).

RQ 5: How is the Perceived Semantic Quality of the model?

5.1 : Does the model represent the facility correctly?
5.2 : Are all elements relevant for the representation of the facility?
5.3 : Does the model give a complete representation of the facility?
5.4 : Does the model contain contradicting elements?
5.5 : Is the model a realistic representation of the facility?

6.3   Results

This section describes the results we derived from the guided interview. The answers of the participants are shown in Table 3.

Table 3. Results from the Guided Interview.

Question	1.1	1.2	1.3	2.1	2.2	2.3	2.4	3.1	3.2	3.3	3.4	4.1	4.2	4.3	4.4	5.1	5.2	5.3	5.4	5.5
Answer	+	+	+	+	+	+	+	+	+	N	+	N	–	+	+	+	+	+	+	+

"+" = Good, "N" = Neutral, "–" = Bad.

- **Modeling Session:** The participants were satisfied with the conduct of the session. 50 min to create a model is perceived as a really good time for both. Answering questions or thinking aloud while working with the tool was no problem. The collaboration was productive and easy, as the participants worked together for a longer time.
- **Graphical Notation:** Both participants perceived the graphical notation as really good. The number of different elements is appropriate, and it is easy to distinguish between them. Different visualizations depend on the types of components, and the use of text is perceived as really helpful, as well as the possibility to rotate the objects in the model. Since the visualizations were co-developed by the employees and mainly originate from a standard they are familiar with, it is not surprising that they have an intuitive effect on them. The only criticism is that some elements seem a bit old-fashioned and could be presented a bit nicer.
- **Process of Model Creation:** The process of creating a model is perceived as perfect for the participants because the tool's functions save time and avoid mistakes. It was easy to place the elements in the correct position and to connect them. The process is more effective now that there is always the same procedure. You don't forget things so easily. The configuration data query could be improved by navigating back and forth between the dialog boxes. This way, errors that were noticed directly can be corrected more quickly. In addition, the note function should be usable during the process of data input.
- **Tool Impression:** The tool was perceived as good but had the potential for further improvements. The bar of the modeling elements could be bigger, so it is easier to identify the elements. It was easy to use the tool's functions, but the menu was confusing in some areas because of the many icons and items. The surface looks very old. So, the overall visualizations could be improved. It would be quite easy to integrate this tool into daily business. Two to four potential employees will be working with it, and it will be easy to teach the tool handling. One participant said that collaborative work with the tool must be made easier in the future. The Export of the file of a model is not intuitive, and in some cases, it will be necessary to send them. For the participants, it makes sense to integrate further functions into the tool, which have been implemented elsewhere so far (e.g., show the status of the sensors in the tool or diagrams of measured/calculated values). The possibilities of exports can be further expanded (e.g., a specific export for the maintenance team).
- **Perceived Semantic Quality:** The answers show that there is agreement between the actor's interpretation of the model and their domain knowledge. The criteria of correctness, relevancy, completeness, consistency, and realism are fulfilled, and thus, the goals of perceived validity and perceived completeness are also fulfilled. In [11], Maes and Poels have shown that the Perceived Semantic Quality influences the user's perception of usefulness and satisfaction. The user's overall satisfaction is further proven to be influenced by the perceived usefulness. During the development of our DSML and tool support, we observed these correlations, which are supported by the interview results.

The importance of the tool for energetic inspections and the valuation of facilities is perceived as very high. It offers many facilitations, allows the digitization of (existing) facilities, and replaces the drawing of models by hand. The consistent process of creating models, supportive functions, and the capability for dynamic adjustments ease the user's work, save time, and avoid mistakes. Explaining the tool to colleagues would be easy. The focus is on explaining the meanings of the individual configuration data that are queried.

7 Summary and Outlook

Our presented DSML, in combination with the tool support, allows the modeling of air conditioning facilities and supports the configuration of IoT applications. The performed quality evaluation based on SEQUAL as a framework demonstrates coherence with the Physical, Syntactic, Semantic, Perceived Semantic, Technical Pragmatic, and Deontic Quality. Empirical and Social (Pragmatic) Quality are partly confirmed by the evaluation, leading to the idea of comparing models from different modelers in the future and involving further actors.

Evaluation of the notation based on Moody's principles proved useful as it resulted in several proposals on how to improve the notation. The most crucial improvement probably is changing the sensor symbol into a new symbol in combination with a relation to the component the sensor is integrated into. However, some of the identified points will not be implemented due to the requirements of our domain or because they conflict with other principles.

In future work, we also have to investigate if differentiation between various user groups (e.g., the designer of the facility and the technician) could lead to an improved Cognitive Fit of the DSML for each user group. However, this requires the involvement of the different groups, a change of the DSML, and - most importantly - thorough evaluation if this really results in positive effects.

The participants evaluation of the language and tool support indicated that the tool is highly valuable. They also expressed their willingness to use it in the future. The participants' answers confirm that modeling is easily possible for domain experts without modeling experience and special IT skills, and the tool functionalities improve and speed up the processes. Tool functionality could be expanded to include, for example, displaying sensor status or collaborative working on models. Additionally, there is potential for improving the tool's appearance and in querying the configuration data.

The main limitation of the practical evaluation is that we only investigated one air conditioning facility. Generalization from this case to several other cases is not reasonably possible. Further, one participant did the modeling in the modeling session, and the other assisted. In practice, it will often be the case that only one employee can take care of the initial modeling. More case studies are needed to ensure the validity and generalizability of the DSML and the tool. In future studies, we recommend also interviewing independent subjects who were not involved in the modeling process.

References

1. Boren, T., Ramey, J.: Thinking aloud: reconciling theory and practice. IEEE Trans. Prof. Commun. **43**(3), 261–278 (2000)
2. Bork, D.: Metamodel-based analysis of domain-specific conceptual modeling methods. In: Buchmann, R.A., Karagiannis, D., Kirikova, M. (eds.) PoEM 2018. LNBIP, vol. 335, pp. 172–187. Springer, Cham (2018). https://doi.org/10.1007/978-3-030-02302-7_11
3. Brambilla, M., Cabot, J., Wimmer, M.: Model-driven software engineering in practice. Synth. Lect. Softw. Eng. **3**(1), 1–207 (2017)
4. Ciccozzi, F., Spalazzese, R.: MDE4IoT: supporting the internet of things with model-driven engineering. In: IDC 2016. SCI, vol. 678, pp. 67–76. Springer, Cham (2017). https://doi.org/10.1007/978-3-319-48829-5_7
5. Döring, N., Bortz, J.: Forschungsmethoden und Evaluation in den Sozial- und Humanwissenschaften. Springer, Berlin (2016). https://doi.org/10.1007/978-3-642-41089-5
6. Frank, U.: Domain-specific modeling languages: Requirements analysis and design guidelines. In: Reinhartz-Berger, I., Sturm, A., Clark, T., Cohen, S., Bettin, J. (eds.) Domain Engineering: Product Lines, Languages, and Conceptual Models, pp. 133–157. Springer, Berlin, Heidelberg (2013). https://doi.org/10.1007/978-3-642-36654-3_6
7. Karagiannis, D., Kühn, H.: Metamodelling platforms. In: Bauknecht, K., Tjoa, A.M., Quirchmayr, G. (eds.) EC-Web 2002. LNCS, vol. 2455, pp. 182–182. Springer, Heidelberg (2002). https://doi.org/10.1007/3-540-45705-4_19
8. Kim, W., Katipamula, S.: A review of fault detection and diagnostics methods for building systems. Sci. Technol. Built Environ. **24**(1), 3–21 (2018)
9. Krogstie, J.: Quality of Business Process Models. Springer, Heidelberg (2016). https://doi.org/10.1007/978-3-319-42512-2
10. Lindland, O.I., Sindre, G., Sølvberg, A.: Understanding quality in conceptual modeling. IEEE Softw. **11**(2), 42–49 (1994)
11. Maes, A., Poels, G.: Evaluating quality of conceptual modelling scripts based on user perceptions. Data Knowl. Eng. **63**(3), 701–724 (2007)
12. Melgaard, S., Andersen, K., Marszal-Pomianowska, A., Jensen, R., Heiselberg, P.: Fault detection and diagnosis encyclopedia for building systems: a systematic review. Energies **15**(12), 4366 (2022)
13. Moody, D.: The "physics" of notations: toward a scientific basis for constructing visual notations in software engineering. IEEE Trans. Software Eng. **35**(6), 756–779 (2009)
14. Nast, B., Sandkuhl, K.: Meta-model and tool support for the organizational aspects of internet-of-things development methods: organizational aspects of IoT development methods. In: Proceedings of the 3rd International Conference on Advanced Information Science and System, pp. 1–6 (2021)
15. Nast., B., Sandkuhl., K.: Methods for model-driven development of IoT applications: requirements from industrial practice. In: Proceedings of the 18th International Conference on Evaluation of Novel Approaches to Software Engineering (ENASE 2023), pp. 170–181 (2023)
16. Nast, B., Sandkuhl, K., Paulus, S., Schiller, H.: MIoTA: modeling IoT applications for air conditioning facilities with ADOxx. In: BIR 2023 Workshops and Doctoral Consortium, 22nd International Conference on Perspectives in Business Informatics Research (BIR 2023), pp. 158–168 (2023)

17. Nelson, H.J., Poels, G., Genero, M., Piattini, M.: A conceptual modeling quality framework. Software Qual. J. **20**, 201–228 (2012)
18. OMiLAB: the ADOxx metamodelling platform. https://www.adoxx.org/live/home. Accessed 11 Oct 2023
19. Poels, G., Maes, A., Gailly, F., Paemeleire, R.: Measuring the perceived semantic quality of information models. In: Akoka, J., et al. (eds.) ER 2005. LNCS, vol. 3770, pp. 376–385. Springer, Heidelberg (2005). https://doi.org/10.1007/11568346_41
20. Sandkuhl, K., Seigerroth, U.: Method engineering in information systems analysis and design: a balanced scorecard approach for method improvement. Softw. Syst. Model. **18**, 1833–1857 (2019)
21. Sosa-Reyna, C.M., Tello-Leal, E., Lara-Alabazares, D.: Methodology for the model-driven development of service oriented IoT applications. J. Syst. Architect. **90**, 15–22 (2018)
22. Wand, Y., Weber, R.: An ontological model of an information system. IEEE Trans. Software Eng. **16**(11), 1282–1292 (1990)

Rapid REST API Management
in a DEMO Based Low Code Platform

Valentim Caires[1,2]([✉]) [iD], João Vasconcelos[1,2] [iD], Duarte Pinto[1,2] [iD],
Vítor Freitas[1,3] [iD], and David Aveiro[1,2,3] [iD]

[1] ARDITI - Regional Agency for the Development of Research,
Technology and Innovation, 9020-105 Funchal, Portugal
{valentim.caires,duarte.nuno,vitor.freitas}@arditi.pt,
2041916@student.uma.pt, daveiro@staff.uma.pt
[2] NOVA-LINCS, Universidade NOVA de Lisboa, Campus da Caparica,
2829-516 Caparica, Portugal
[3] Faculty of Exact Sciences and Engineering, University of Madeira,
Caminho da Penteada, 9020-105 Funchal, Portugal

Abstract. In enterprise data management, the development of APIs
for integrating diverse information systems often entails repetitive and
labor-intensive tasks, such as translating variables and methods between
systems. The advent of low-code platforms has significantly altered this
landscape, facilitating the automatic and swift generation of APIs for
both incoming and outgoing data and service actions. This paper explores
a new approach using the Design and Engineering Methodology for
Organizations (DEMO) data models within a low-code platform. Our
methodology simplifies the API creation process by using DEMO's Fact
and Action models. Using a low-code platform, we enable users to effi-
ciently generate endpoints for various functionalities, ranging from basic
data item lists to complex query results, all achieved through intuitive
drag-and-drop operations within a user-friendly graphical interface. This
approach not only streamlines the development of APIs for internal tasks
but also eases integration with external systems. Moreover, our approach
includes the automated scanning of data from external APIs. Utilizing
a user-friendly GUI, our system can automatically retrieve data from
external sources and align it with internal data, ensuring consistent integration. This paper details this approach, emphasizing its effectiveness
in integrating external information into local systems.

Keywords: Low-Code Platforms · DEMO · Model Driven · REST
API · Enterprise Engineering · External API Integration

1 Introduction

In enterprise data management, using REST APIs as backend web services has
become a prevalent strategy. REST APIs provide programmatic access to services and data within applications or databases, adhering to specific architectural

constraints. However, backend software development presents considerable challenges, requiring detailed attention to data integrity, confidentiality, availability, and privacy, along with the ability to handle multiple requests concurrently. Implementing such services requires extensive expertise.

This paper has, as context, the research initiative Dynamic Information System Modeller and Executor (DISME) [1], a low-code open-source software platform based on Design and Engineering Methodology for Organizations (DEMO) methodology. Our specific focus hereby presented, is on the challenge of rapidly and automatically generating and managing inbound and outbound REST interfaces using the DEMO way of modeling approach [2], facilitated through a low-code platform. Our goal is to enable managers and individuals in similar roles within organizations to create and oversee REST API endpoints, eventually with no need of programming skills.

Low-code platforms offer a viable solution for the rapid and automatic generation of APIs, covering both incoming and outgoing data and service actions. By leveraging data models within a low-code information system, the creation of endpoints—ranging from basic data item lists to the results of complex queries—becomes accessible through intuitive drag-and-drop operations within a user-friendly graphical interface. This platform not only allows execution of internal tasks based on external system requests but also facilitates the scanning of data from external APIs, aligning it with internal data and rules.

This paper expands the Rapid REST API Management (RRAM) approach [3], deeply rooted in the DEMO methodology [2]. A key component of DISME, the Action Rules specification, harnesses Blockly[1], a visual code editor that simplifies the configuration of business rules following a formal Extended Backus Naur Form (EBNF) grammar. Blockly's graphical blocks represent fundamental code concepts, enabling users to apply programming principles without grappling with syntax complexities. Building upon our expertise with Blockly, we are developing this RRAM component for DISME, enabling the management of inbound and outbound API interfaces through an intuitive GUI. Notably, this component not only facilitates the (semi-)automatic generation of API configurations and data formats but also automates documentation creation using Swagger UI[2]

2   Literature Review

In this section, we provide a review of existing research related to the (automatic) generation, management, and documentation of REST APIs.

Some researchers have explored code generation approaches. Wang et al. [4] introduced a model-based method for generating code to access databases, which was then encapsulated into RESTful APIs. While this approach minimizes efforts

---

[1] Blockly - https://developers.google.com/blockly.

[2] Swagger UI - https://swagger.io/tools/swagger-ui.

and enhances flexibility and reusability, it also comes with multiple drawbacks such as significant initial efforts, code rigidity, and increased technical complexity.

Other studies advocate Model-driven Engineering (MDE) [5,6] as an iterative and incremental software development process. Mora-Segura et al. [5] proposed a solution based on multi-level modeling representing domain knowledge. It supports on-demand data loading through domain injectors, described by semantic-rich query descriptions.

Hussein et al. [7] developed REST API Automatic Generation (RAAG), an integrated framework abstracting layers for REST APIs, business logic, data access, and model operations. RAAG, designed for reusability, maintainability, scalability, and performance, significantly reduced development time compared to traditional REST API implementations, as evidenced by a preliminary evaluation. Users, including non-experienced developers, found RAAG intuitive, maintainable, and productive, highlighting its ease-of-use and efficiency.

Overeem et al. [8] evaluated API management maturity in major low-code development platforms (LCDPs). Challenges arose in making APIs accessible to inexperienced users due to the inherent simplification of LCDPs conflicting with the complexity of software solutions. Striking a balance between simplicity and functionality is crucial.

Brajesh De [9] emphasized the importance of user-friendly API documentation for the successful adoption of REST APIs. The documentation should offer an easy-to-understand interface, enabling developers, regardless of their experience, to comprehend the API's features and seamlessly start using it.

Additionally, in [10], an algorithm was proposed for generating micro-services conforming to the OpenAPI standard from a DEMO ontological model. However, the approach generates services for all transaction acts, which is excessive. Furthermore, implementation limitations, such as defining value types and DELETE operations, were encountered. Addressing these issues, it was noted that while, ontologically, facts cannot be changed or deleted, practical implementations require such capabilities, considering regulations like European GDPR. Our proposed solution aims to overcome these limitations.

Despite diverse studies on REST API generation and management, some methods rely on complex tools or demand specific experience, limiting their accessibility. Some lack support for various databases, only allowing data retrieval, while others primarily focus on code generation [4]. However, it is evident from the evaluated papers [4,6] that (semi-)automatic generation of REST APIs is a viable option. Properly executed, this approach simplifies the process, enabling individuals with limited programming experience to participate. Equally significant is the emphasis on creating user-friendly API documentation, ensuring both experienced and inexperienced users can understand and utilize the API effectively.

3   DEMO Models

Building upon the foundational concepts of Design and Engineering Methodology for Organizations (DEMO) [2], our innovative approach to automatic API generation builds on the latest advancements in DEMO Models. These advancements, detailed in [1, 3, 11–17], represent a paradigm shift in their user-friendly approach when contrasted with traditional methods [2]. Let us explore the key components in detail:

3.1   Fact Model (FM) and Fact Diagram (FD)

At the heart of DEMO lies the Fact Model (FM) [13], aiming to represent an organization's products and services. The FM defines an organization's state and transition spaces within the production world [2]. A relevant artifact within FM is the Fact Diagram (FD), which provides insights through two lenses: the Concept and Relationships Diagram (CRD) and the Concept Attribute Diagram (CAD).

In the CRD, relationships are portrayed using arrows, symbolizing attributes in one concept that link to instances in another. This visual representation clearly shows the dependencies between concepts. Notably, binary fact types are categorized into three distinct relationships: one-to-one, many-to-one, and many-to-many, each distinguished by specific symbols. For instance, one-to-one relationships feature connectors with dual arrows, denoting exclusivity.

The CAD, an extension of CRD, carefully outlines concepts' attributes. Each concept is encapsulated within a collapsible box, detailing its attributes and corresponding value types. This detailed breakdown enhances the comprehension of concept properties [11, 13].

3.2   Action Model (AM) and Action Rule Specification (ARS)

DEMO's Action Model [12] comprises the organization's operations, guiding actors through transaction coordination acts. Action rules are specified to direct actors in their roles. What sets DEMO apart is its adherence to communicative rationality, allowing actors the flexibility to adapt their behavior based on professional judgment and expertise.

The evolution of Action Rule Specification (ARS) languages has been a key factor in ensuring clarity and accuracy. The contemporary ARS encompasses three vital elements: the event (coordinated actions), assess (validity claims), and response (action instructions), which brings unneeded complexity and lack of precision. In [16] we have proposed an alternative ARS language, formalized with EBNF. In Fig. 1, we present an example of an Action Rule in Blockly. This new approach integrates expressions, logical conditions, validations, input forms, and templated-document outputs. By streamlining the syntax, it enhances practical application and functionality needed for our RRAM approach.

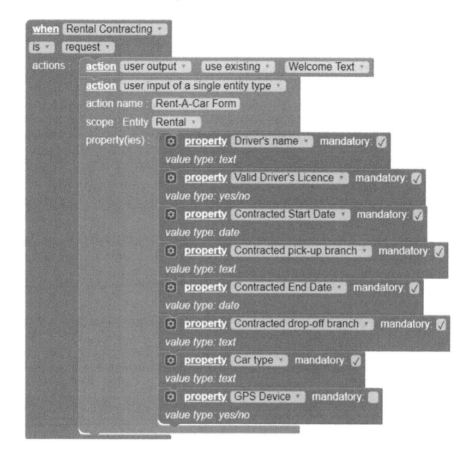

Fig. 1. Action rule for the request of "Rental Contracting" transaction

4 Our Low-Code Platform Approach

The Rapid REST API Management (RRAM) component is being developed as part of DISME, which comprises two main components:

1. **The System Modeler:** a comprehensive toolset within DISME, enabling users to describe organizational artifacts effectively. It includes:
   (a) **Diagram Editor**, which allows visual representation of processes through DEMO models, automating database entries and enhancing design [1].
   (b) **The System Specifier** that simplifies the management of model elements, roles, processes, transactions, and entity types, eliminating the need for programming skills [1].
   (c) **Action Rules Management** that utilizes structured English and Blockly to specify process logic and inputs, streamlining complex business rule creation without extensive programming knowledge [1].

(d) **Forms Management** integrates Form.io for seamless form creation, ensuring precise alignment between specified inputs and user-filled forms [1].

(e) **Dynamic Query Management** component that empowers users to create queries effortlessly through a graphical interface, utilizing property-operator-value triplets. This feature enables dynamic and flexible data retrieval, accommodating diverse information needs [1].

2. **System Executor:** Facilitates the direct execution of the modeled information system in production mode. It consists of the Dashboard, providing the user interface for organizational tasks, and the Execution Engine, ensuring information and process flow aligns with the system's specifications [1].

DISME progress has been validated through the application of these functionalities to the NexusBRaNT case [18].

The RRAM approach capitalizes on the ongoing DISME development and DEMO methodology to generate endpoints, accessible both within the local system and externally. The goal was to seamlessly integrate rapid and/or semi-automatic REST API generation and handling into DISME, an evolving system. RRAM is being built upon existing features such as Action Rule specification and the complex query modeling, developed through Blockly and jQuery Query-Builder[3], that gives it a strong foundation. Extending these components by utilizing existing information such as business facts, attributes, action rules, and queries, will complement the creation of a dedicated component for modeling and specifying REST API endpoints.

To address our research challenge, we outline four primary functionalities necessary for seamless integration with other systems through REST APIs. These functionalities encompass:

- **Simple CRUD Operations:** This involves Create, Read, Update, and Delete operations on data from the local DISME system. These operations are facilitated through intuitive interfaces, allowing users to specify the data to be exposed via the API. The complexity of these operations is mitigated as each operation involves a single concept from the system.
- **Query-Based Data Provision:** DISME facilitates query-based data provision, allowing users to retrieve specific datasets based on their requirements.
- **Integrating internal execution with external endpoint calls:** This functionality involves aligning internal action rules and corresponding local data with data required from external systems.
- **Enabling internal execution by local endpoint calls:** DISME matches local endpoints provided to external systems with internal action rules, ensuring seamless integration.

API endpoint details, including HTTP methods, parameters, and response fields, are inferred from their specifications within our system. This information not only specifies the endpoint but also auto-generates API documentation, facilitated through Swagger UI.

---

[3] jQuery QueryBuilder - https://querybuilder.js.org/.

4.1 Simple CRUD Operations

This facet involved creating endpoints for Create, Read, Update, and Delete operations for each of DISME's internal concept/entity types. These operations are straightforward as they involve only one concept from the system, reducing their complexity. DISME offers an interface enabling users to select the information to expose via the API, including specific entity type properties/attributes for CRUD operations. These selections are stored in the DISME's database tables, automatically generating the corresponding endpoints.

4.2 Query Based Data Providing

In scenarios where simple CRUD operations fall short, DISME offers another solution, the association of complex queries with specific endpoints. We developed an intuitive interface enabling users to configure complex queries almost effortlessly. This component operates on the principle of specifying queries and their filters through triplets of property-operator-value, all selected via drag-and-drop actions in a user-friendly graphical interface, eliminating the need for any programming expertise.

In the first step, users select the entity types focused on in the search as seen in Fig. 2, with the initial selection serving as the Base Table—the entity type where the search for entity values occurs based on defined filters.

Fig. 2. Query interface - Step 1 - Select Entity Type.

The second step involves defining the query's properties. For each selected entity type, users specify the properties to be included in the result as well as properties to be used in the filters, as seen in Fig. 3.

These selected properties form the basis for specifying triplets of property-operator-value in step three. There, users define rules and rule sets that are applied to the main query, akin to conditions and sub-conditions. Users choose

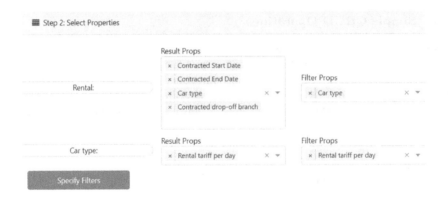

Fig. 3. Query interface - Step 2 - Select Properties.

the type of rule (and/or), the property to be filtered, the query's operator, and the value restricting the result as seen in Fig. 4.

Fig. 4. Query interface - Step 3 - Specify Filters.

Configured queries as seen in Fig. 5, with clearly specified result properties, facilitate the configuration of API endpoints whose responses align with the query results. Users can view the list of properties related to a query and select the relevant ones to be included in the API response. This also applies to filters; users can specify one or more filters as query parameters, leaving the values to be assigned at runtime—for instance, when an endpoint is called with specific parameter values.

It's important to note that the DISME's database uses tables with names: entity type and property for specifying the enterprise's data model, yet in DISME's user interface, we utilize the names: concept and attribute, from the adapted DEMO's FM meta-model, corresponding to entity type and property, respectively.

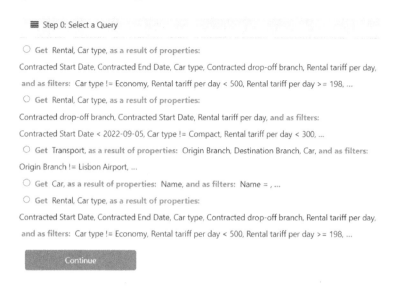

Fig. 5. Configured Queries.

4.3 Integrating Internal Execution with External Endpoint Calls

For the integration of internal execution and external endpoints calls, a series of tasks had to be undertaken, the first part was the creation of the new internal actions. This was achieved with the addiction of several new elements to the grammar and respective blocks to Blockly and their supporting structure, namely:

- Show Result: An action developed to display external API call results to users through a dedicated interface. This involved creating a new action type within DISME, allowing users to visualize data obtained from external systems.
- Create Entity(ies): Another action type was implemented to import values from external systems into DISME. This required mapping external data to corresponding internal entities and properties, ensuring data integrity within DISME.
- Create Temporary Entity(ies): A specialized action was developed to perform external calls and store temporary data within DISME for user input during the execution of action rules.
- Matching: A component that allows the user to create a correspondence between the properties of the entity selected in the create entity(ies) block and the properties existing in the content of the API call result.
- Temporary Matching: A component similar to matching, but with the responsibility of matching the system's properties with the properties returned by the REST API.

The second task was to modify the REST API component, to accommodate the new necessities, namely by creating the API Request Service to facilitate external API calls. This service allowed configuration of common parameters such as headers, URL, request body content, and request type (POST, GET, PUT, DELETE). This abstraction reduced code duplication and enhanced system modularity. It also accommodates the Integration Logic, by making sure the REST API component was properly integrated with DISME's internal logic. This involved creating a communication bridge between the DISME backend and external systems.

And to conclude the second task, handling external responses, a component was designed to handle responses from external systems, which could be in JSON or XML format. DISME processes these responses, allowing users to interact with the retrieved data.

The last task was data management, namely create a temporary data storage to handle temporary data from external systems, a strategy was devised to store this data within temporary tables in the DISME's database. This ensured that external data could be utilized within the DISME context without compromising the overall system integrity.

The Form Generation and User Input allows the DISME dynamically generated forms for user input based on temporary data. These forms allowed users to interact with and validate external data before incorporating it into the DISME's internal structure.

Finally, it specifies the mapping and correspondence by implementing mechanisms to map external properties to internal properties, allowing seamless integration of temporary data. This mapping ensured that temporary data could be utilized effectively within DISME's entities and properties.

With these three tasks it was possible to integrate internal execution with external endpoint calls in REST API component. In Fig. 6 we have an example of configuration of an external API call.

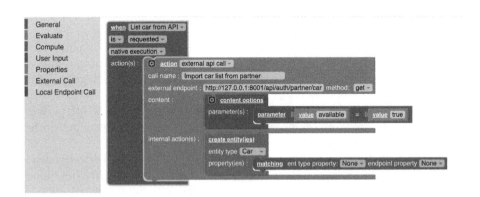

Fig. 6. Example of configuring an *external API call*.

4.4 Enabling Internal Execution by Local Endpoint Calls

In order to enable the implementation of local endpoints for creating new objects, we first needed to develop the new Blockly blocks that will contain/request all the information that is required to properly create an endpoint, in the form of internal action rules, as well as some additional information to create the respective documentation.

The information required for each endpoint is the following, but some of them may be deduced or be used to deduce each other:

- HTTP method
- URI
- URI parameters
- Endpoint name
- The listing of attributes of the object to be created, each attribute containing:
  - name of the attribute
  - description of the attribute
  - entity type
  - value type (number, text, date,...)
  - restrictions and/or validations (e.g. check if a number is greater than 0)
  - an example of a possible value for this attribute
  - mark the attribute as mandatory or optional
- The action(s) to be executed:
  - creating the database records, by matching each endpoint attribute with the corresponding entity type attribute
- The responses:
  - Success:
    * Generic success message
    * The newly created/updated, queried or deleted object, picking which attributes should be returned
  - Error - depending on the type of error a message is generated accordingly

Although the Action Rules Management Component of DISME already has many customized blocks, we needed to create a few new blocks and/or personalize some of the existing ones to support this new feature. Firstly, the main block, that is used as a starting point to create any action rule, had a new option added: "local endpoint call", which turns the block into a specific template for creating a new endpoint, namely the endpoint's path, the endpoint arguments/parameters, the request body, the action(s) to be executed and the possible responses. The main block, with the "local endpoint call" option selected is shown in Fig. 7.

Then we created a block to collect the information for each parameter, which can be used to set endpoint parameters/arguments, as well as the request body parameters. The information required to complete this block is: name of the parameter, a brief description that is used to create the documentation, the internal entity type, the internal property, an example value for the parameter, a checkbox to determine whether the parameter is mandatory and also, if needed, the option to add "validation condition(s)" can be chosen. If so, it will

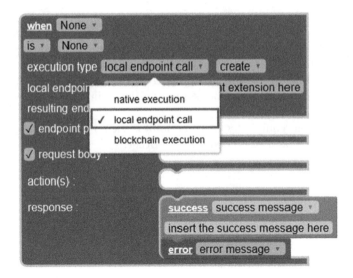

Fig. 7. The starting block, with the new execution type.

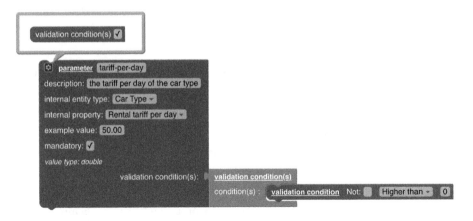

Fig. 8. The "parameter" block with validation condition

be possible to choose one or more validation conditions among a limited list of possible validations based on the value type of the parameter. An example of the "parameter" block can be found in Fig. 8.

If the endpoint has nested objects in the request, there is also the option of using the "parameter set" block, which uses the same "parameter" blocks inside, as shown in Fig. 9.

Then we changed the behavior of the "action" block when it is associated to the block in Fig. 7 and the "local endpoint call" option selected. The "action" block has now the "create record" option selected, and it will allow us to create the database records. In the entity type, we choose which of the existing entities

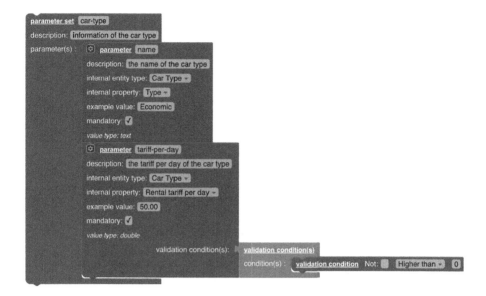

Fig. 9. The "parameter set" block

we are creating a new record and select a checkbox if duplicate records are allowed. In property(ies) we use a new block called "matching" which matches the property of the entity type to the property received as an endpoint parameter. In Fig. 10, an example of the "action" block with two "matching" blocks is presented.

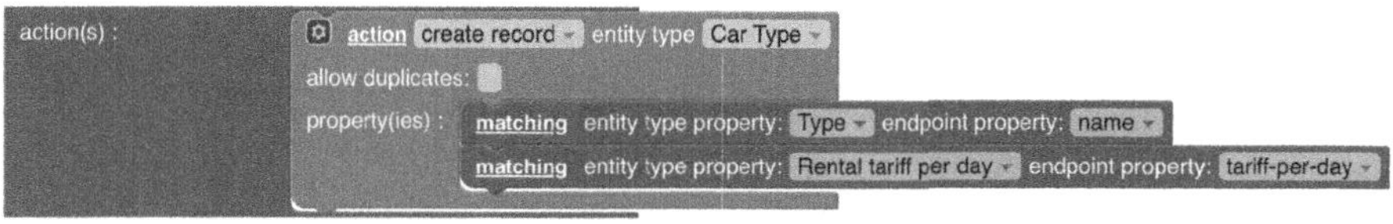

Fig. 10. The "action" block and "matching" blocks

To conclude, we need to configure the response. If there is any error while executing the endpoint, a message and a HTTP status code will be returned accordingly. In case of success, we have the option of sending a generic success message, as shown in Fig. 7, or we can choose to return the newly created object as a response. To do this we select the "created object" option, and then we can add as many "response property" blocks as we need, where we fill in the property name how we want it to be in the response and the internal entity type and property it corresponds to, as shown in Fig. 11. The reason to set these properties instead of deducing them from the request or the entity itself is because the objects may contain more properties that have, perhaps, been generated by the endpoint and also because we might not want to return every property, but only a few of them.

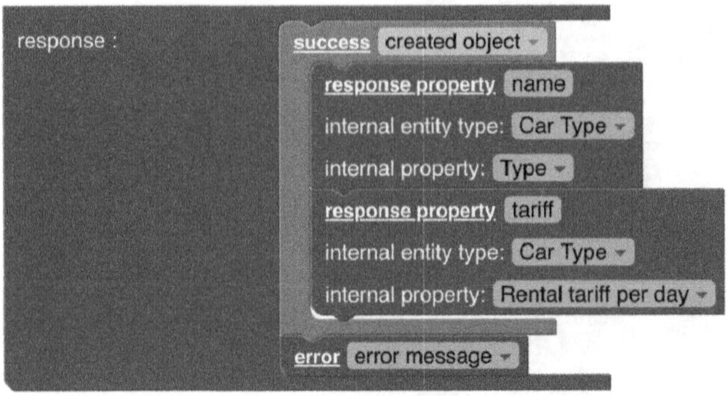

Fig. 11. The "response property" blocks inside the success block

Also, similarly to the "parameter" blocks, it is possible to use the "response set" block to return nested objects, which uses the same "response property" blocks inside, as presented in Fig. 12.

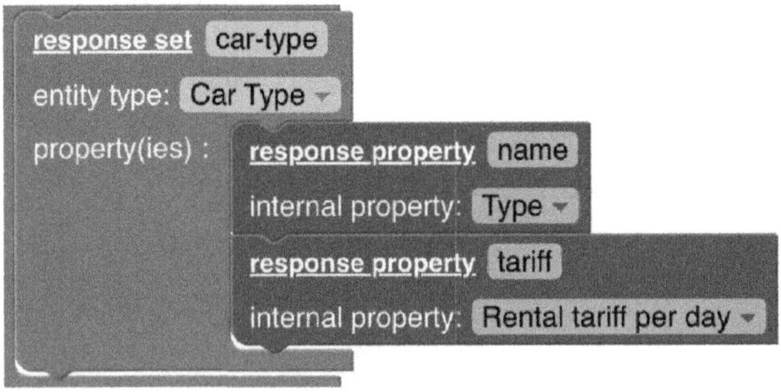

Fig. 12. The "response set" block

4.5   Extending the Action Meta Model's EBNF Grammar

This paper makes an additional contribution by suggesting an extension to the existing EBNF grammar for DISME's action rules. The modifications outlined in this section directly pertain to Subsect. 4.4. In Figs. 13, 14 and 15 presented below, we only specify and subsequently explain the new or updated concepts within DISME's action rule EBNF grammar. This approach is taken to avoid excessive space usage and to maintain the focus on the relevant discussion.

An action rule operates within the context of a predefined transaction type within the system. This rule is activated during a specific transaction state. Our proposal broadens the definition of an action rule by introducing an execution type that is categorized into two distinct modes: native execution, which pertains to the standard execution of action rules through user interactions on the platform's dashboard, and local endpoint call execution, which involves executing the rule through an external system's API call to a defined system endpoint, as previously described.

In the case of defining an action rule with the 'local endpoint call' execution type, as previously shown, it is necessary to specify the local endpoint that external systems will interact with. This is followed by detailing the API call's parameters, which may include mandatory or optional system properties. Finally, one must define the expected response from the call. This allows for the explicit specification of individual properties, including their name and value type. Alternatively, a group of properties can be defined by specifying their names and then selecting them from an entity type within the system.

execution_type	NATIVE_EXECUTION | LOCAL_ENDPOINT_CALL
local_endpoint_call_info	local_endpoint_call_type local_endpoint_path {local_endpoint_parameter} [local_endpoint_request_body] local_endpoint_response
local_endpoint_call_type	CREATE | READ | UPDATE | DELETE NOTE: API Call CRUD operation that will be carried. Influences the action types that will be present in the 'action' block. For 'create', we will have the 'assign expression' and 'create record' action types, for 'read' we will have the 'query ledger' and 'query asset' action types, for 'update' we will have the 'update asset' action type, and for 'delete' we will have the 'delete asset' action type.
local_endpoint_path	STRING NOTE: path that will extend the application's domain. Ex: "/getParcel". The url parameters are automatically inserted after the path by Blockly as they are added into the action rule, originating the resulting endpoint. Ex: "/getParcel/id"
local_endpoint_parameter	STRING property documentation_description parameter_example_value {validation_condition} [MANDATORY] NOTE: the parameter name that will be used to specify the parameter is independent of the internal property that is linked to it, and therefore doesn't have to be the equal to its name.
documentation_description	STRING NOTE: Description of the parameter/parameter_set, needed for the generation of the api endpoint through Swagger.

Fig. 13. EBNF table - Part 1

parameter_example_value	STRING NOTE: An example of the parameter's accepted value. Needed for the generation of the api endpoint through Swagger.
local_endpoint_request_body	{local_endpoint_parameter | local_endpoint_parameter_set}- NOTE: defines the structure of the API Call's reqest_body, defining its parameters and/or parameter_sets.
local_endpoint_parameter_set	STRING documentation_description {local_endpoint_parameter}- NOTE: After specifying the set_name, it is needed to specify the parameters that are to be inserted into it.
local_endpoint_response	local_endpoint_success_response local_endpoint_error_response NOTE: must have a behaviour selected for each one. One defined in case the API call is carried out successfully, and one in case it encounters any errors in the process.
local_endpoint_success_response	local_endpoint_success_response_affected_object | local_endpoint_success_response_queried_object | STRING NOTE: When successful, it can return the created/queried/updated/deleted object or simply a custom success message. NOTE: API Call CRUD operation that will be carried influences the dropdown choices that will be present in the 'response' block. For 'create', we will have the 'created object', for 'read' we will have the 'response_queried_object', for 'update' we will have the 'updated object', and for 'delete' we will have the 'deleted object'. Except for the 'read' crud operation, we have the option to output a custom success message instead of the object.
local_endpoint_success_response_affected_object	STRING {response_property | response_set}- NOTE: defines the returning object with the object's name and the properties/property_sets that should be returned inside it.
response_property	STRING property NOTE: has to be a property belonging to the object that was created/updated/queried/deleted.
response_set	STRING {response_property}- NOTE: defines the set name and the properties that should be included in this response set.
local_endpoint_success_response_queried_object	STRING NOTE: the variable names defined in the 'query records' blocks will appear here in a dropdown and the user must select which ones to include in the api call's response. Will return the objects from the selected queries.

Fig. 14. EBNF table - Part 2

local_endpoint_error_response	STRING NOTE: error message to be returned.
action	causal_link | assign_expression | user_input | edit_entity_instance | user_output | produce_doc | if | while | for_each | post | get | create_record | query_records | update_record | delete_record
set	STRING set of elements NOTE: set of elements. Has to be a name of a 'parameter set' defined in the action rule's 'request body' input.
create_record	entity_type {matching_property}- [ALLOW_DUPLICATES] NOTE: Allows the creation of an entity in the system. 'Allow duplicates' is a checkbox that will/won't allow the insertion of duplicate records of entities of the entity type selected.
entity_type	STRING *NOTE: has to be an existent enttity_type specified in table ent_type*
matching_property	MATCHING property local_endpoint_property NOTE: matches an internal property to an input parameter/property of the API Call defined in the 'local_endpoint_parameter'/ 'local_endpoint_request_body' inputs.
local_endpoint_property	STRING NOTE: has to be a property referenced by a local_endpoint_parameter inside the action rule's definition.
matching_id_property	MATCHING ID_PROPERTY local_endpoint_property NOTE: the only matching_property inserted here is the identifying property of the selected entity type, i.e. the 'id' property. Blockly automatically inserts it into the block as the matching_property's property.
query_records	query [QUERY_DELETED_OBJECTS] NOTE: get query results from the specified query. Blockly will have a dropdown to select the queries currently defined in the system.
update_record	entity_type matching_id_property {matching_property} NOTE: properties to be updated in the entity are the matching_properties inserted. The matching_id_property is to know which entity to update.
delete_record	entity_type matching_id_property NOTE: will search for the selected entity type's entity with the received api call id and will delete that entity.

Fig. 15. EBNF table - Part 3

5   Conclusions and Future Work

In this paper, we have introduced a novel approach to the management of
rapid REST API development using the DEMO methodology and a model-
driven low-code solution. Our solution, embedded within the DISME platform,
offers a methodical way to create and manage APIs. By leveraging and updating
DEMO's Action Meta Model, we enable the automatic or rapid generation of
both incoming and outgoing APIs through an intuitive drag-and-drop interface.

Our approach of combining refined DEMO Action Models with DISME low-
code platforms components, reduces the complexities of API development and
management, reducing the time and effort traditionally required. The automatic

generation of API documentation ensures clarity and improves system maintainability. In line with these advancements, our ongoing efforts will include comprehensive testing, encompassing usability, integration, and performance tests, to ensure the enhanced functionality meets the users' needs effectively.

Building on this foundation, in a specific component of DISME, we allow the development of dynamic query functionalities enabling users to dynamically parameterize queries. This enhancement allows users to define query parameters during execution, enhancing the flexibility and utility of our API management solution.

Future work involves integrating the ability to handle REST requests with dynamic parameters, augmenting the capabilities of the action rules configured in DISME and offered in local endpoints to external systems. Also, currently, we support just simple token authentication methods and REST standard and we plan to support, in the future, more complex authentication methods (and their management too) like OAuth and also the SOAP standard.

References

1. Freitas, V., Pinto, D., Caires, V., Tadeu, L., Aveiro, D.: The DISME low-code platform - from simple diagram creation to system execution. In: Proceedings of the 22nd CIAO! Doctoral Consortium, and Enterprise Engineering Working Conference Forum (2022)
2. Dietz, J., Mulder, H.: Enterprise Ontology: A Human-Centric Approach to Understanding the Essence of Organisation. Springer International Publishing, The Enterprise Engineering Series (2020). https://doi.org/10.1007/978-3-030-38854-6
3. Aveiro, D., Caires, V.: DEMO model based rapid REST API management in a low code platform. In: Guerreiro, S., Griffo, C., Jacob, M. (eds.) Proceedings of the 22nd CIAO! Doctoral Consortium, and Enterprise Engineering Working Conference Forum 2022 co-located with 12th Enterprise Engineering Working Conference (EEWC 2022), November 2-3, 2022, Leusden, the Netherlands. CEUR Workshop Proceedings, CEUR-WS.org, vol. 3388 (2022)
4. Wang, B., Rosenberg, D., Boehm, B.W.: Rapid realization of executable domain models via automatic code generation. In: 2017 IEEE 28th Annual Software Technology Conference (STC), pp. 1–6 (2017)
5. Segura, A.M., Cuadrado, J.S., De Lara, J.: ODaaS: towards the model-driven engineering of open data applications as data services. In: 2014 IEEE 18th International Enterprise Distributed Object Computing Conference Workshops and Demonstrations, pp. 335–339 (2014)
6. da Cruz Gonçalves, R.C.: RESTful web services development with a model-driven engineering approach. PhD thesis, Instituto Superior de Engenharia do Porto (2018). AAI28992236
7. Hussein, S. Zein, S., Salleh, N.: Rest API auto generation: a model-based approach. In: Knowledge Innovation Through Intelligent Software Methodologies, Tools and Techniques, p. 09 (2020)
8. Overeem, M., Jansen, S., Mathijssen, M.: API management maturity of low-code development platforms. In: Augusto, A., Gill, A., Nurcan, S., Reinhartz-Berger, I., Schmidt, R., Zdravkovic, J. (eds.) BPMDS/EMMSAD -2021. LNBIP, vol. 421, pp. 380–394. Springer, Cham (2021). https://doi.org/10.1007/978-3-030-79186-5_25

9. De, B.: API Management: An Architect's Guide to Developing and Managing APIs for Your Organization. Apress (2017)
10. Krouwel, M.R., Op 't Land, M.: Business driven microservice design. In: Aveiro, D., Proper, H.A., Guerreiro, S., de Vries, M. (eds.) Advances in Enterprise Engineering XV, pp. 95–113. Springer, Cham (2022). https://doi.org/10.1007/978-3-031-11520-2_7
11. Andrade, M., Aveiro, D., Pinto, D.: Bridging ontology and implementation with a new DEMO action meta-model and engine. In: Aveiro, D., Guizzardi, G., Borbinha, J. (eds.) EEWC 2019. LNBIP, vol. 374, pp. 66–82. Springer, Cham (2020). https://doi.org/10.1007/978-3-030-37933-9_5
12. Pinto, D., Aveiro, D., Pacheco, D., Gouveia, B., Gouveia, D.: Validation of DEMO's conciseness quality and proposal of improvements to the process model. In: Aveiro, D., Guizzardi, G., Pergl, R., Proper, H.A. (eds.) EEWC 2020. LNBIP, vol. 411, pp. 133–152. Springer, Cham (2021). https://doi.org/10.1007/978-3-030-74196-9_8
13. Gouveia, B., Aveiro, D., Pacheco, D., Pinto, D., Gouveia, D.: Fact model in DEMO - urban law case and proposal of representation improvements. In: Aveiro, D., Guizzardi, G., Pergl, R., Proper, H.A. (eds.) EEWC 2020. LNBIP, vol. 411, pp. 173–190. Springer, Cham (2021). https://doi.org/10.1007/978-3-030-74196-9_10
14. Pacheco, D., Aveiro, D., Pinto, D., Gouveia, B.: Towards the x-theory: an evaluation of the perceived quality and functionality of demo's process model. In: Aveiro, D. Proper, H.A., Guerreiro, S., de Vries, M. (eds.) Advances in Enterprise Engineering XV, pp. 129–148. Springer, Cham (2022). https://doi.org/10.1007/978-3-031-11520-2_9
15. Pacheco, D., Aveiro, D., Gouveia, B., Pinto, D.: Evaluation of the perceived quality and functionality of fact model diagrams in DEMO. In: Aveiro, D., Proper, H.A., Guerreiro, S., de Vries, M. (eds.) Advances in Enterprise Engineering XV, Lecture Notes in Business Information Processing, pp. 114–128. Springer, Cham (2022). https://doi.org/10.1007/978-3-031-11520-2_8
16. Aveiro, D., Freitas, V.: A new action meta-model and grammar for a DEMO based low-code platform rules processing engine. In: Griffo, C., Guerreiro, S., Iacob, M.E. (eds.) Advances in Enterprise Engineering XVI, Lecture Notes in Business Information Processing, pp. 33–52. Springer, Cham (2023). https://doi.org/10.1007/978-3-031-34175-5_3
17. Aveiro, D., Oliveira, J.: Towards DEMO model-based automatic generation of smart contracts. In: Griffo, C., Guerreiro, S., Iacob, M.E. (eds.) Advances in Enterprise Engineering XVI, Lecture Notes in Business Information Processing, pp. 71–89. Springer, Cham (2023). https://doi.org/10.1007/978-3-031-34175-5_5
18. Aveiro, D., Freitas, V., Cunha, E., Quintal, F., Almeida, Y.: Traditional vs. low-code development: comparing needed effort and system complexity in the Nexus-BRaNT experiment. In: 2023 IEEE 25th Conference on Business Informatics (CBI), pp. 1–10 (2023)

On the Concept of Discovery Power of Enterprise Modeling Languages and Its Relation to Their Expressive Power

Ilia Bider[1,2][✉] [iD] and Erik Perjons[1] [iD]

[1] Stockholm University, Borgarfjordsgatan 12, Kista, 164 55 Stockholm, Sweden
{ilia,perjons}@dsv.su.se
[2] University of Tartu, Ülikooli 18, 50090 Tartu, Estonia

Abstract. The paper introduces a new concept – discovery power – that can be used to characterize an enterprise modeling language. The concept is different from, but connected to, the concept of expressive power. The concept is defined as "the degree of help provided by the structure of an enterprise modeling language to expand a partly built model or fill gaps in it". The paper also suggests a way of evaluating the discovery power of enterprise modeling languages.

Keywords: Discovery power · Expressive power · Enterprise model · OODA

1 Introduction

The term *Expressive Power* of a language, especially an artificial language, was introduced quite a long time ago for programming languages, see [1], which is from 1991. The informal definition of the concept applied to a language in general in Wikipedia sounds like "the breadth of ideas that can be represented and communicated in that language" [2]. This definition needs to be more precise to be used in practice, e.g., for comparing the expressive power of two candidate languages. Therefore, several more exact definitions of the concept were created for specific kinds of languages. For example, for workflow-based modeling languages, patterns are used to evaluate the expressive power of a workflow language [3]. The language that formally expresses all possible patterns has the best expressive power. In the domain of programming languages [4], the language that allows defining a solution in terms of the problem rather than in terms of an abstract machine is considered to have a greater expressive power. This means that the expressive power can, for example, be defined as a length of code to express a particular algorithm. That is, the language requiring less code has a greater expressive power with regard to a certain kind of algorithms.

In this paper, we are investigating enterprise modeling languages in relation to their usage for helping humans decide on the course of action, i.e., the area of application of modeling is human-based decision-making. It means that the interpreters of the models are people, not machines. Based on our experience, the model used in such a situation does not need to be formally correct to be useful. Also, a human's understanding of the

M. Malinova Mandelburger et al. (Eds.): EDEWC 2023, LNBIP 510, pp. 92–106, 2024.
https://doi.org/10.1007/978-3-031-58935-5_6

model to a high degree depends on the labels assigned to its modeling elements; the labels need to be meaningful to the decision makers that would use the model. Therefore, a model created in a modeling language with a few concepts can still be useful if the labels are chosen carefully. Still, with equally good labels, some models can be more useful, as they highlight essential elements by using special means that exist in the language.

The expressive power is not the only modeling language characteristic that should be taken into consideration when deciding which language to use. In this paper, we introduce another characteristic that does not exist in the research literature: *discovery power*. The importance of this characteristic depends on the context of the project in which the model is created. If all information needed to build a model is already known, the discovery power of the modeling language is not relevant to the project, while the expressive power is. In such a case, the main point is to be able to express all vital information by means of the language. When the information needed to build a model is unavailable beforehand, the discovery power can be of importance. Informally, the discovery power can be defined as "help that the structure of the modeling language provides for identifying elements of reality to be depicted in the model". As an example of discovery power, consider the specialization relation that exists in many modeling languages. When some object/class has been identified and put in the model, e.g., a customer, this relation can be used to investigate whether there are different types of customers, e.g., private and organizational customers.

The situation when the discovery power is relevant for the project is determined by the relation between the modeler or modeling team and the enterprise that should be depicted in the model. If the modeler or team has experience in modeling a similar enterprise, the discovery power of the language might not be important. However, if the enterprise is in the domain where the modelers do not have experience, choosing a language with substantial discovery power can help to build a relevant model or, in a lesser case, minimize the time and other resources needed for building the model. Even the latter is essential for practice, as the resources allocated to a modeling project, including the time the stakeholders answer the questions, are always limited.

Help from the structure of the modeling language is not the only source for unearthing the information needed for building the model. There are other methods to discover information to build a model, like modeling patterns [5]. However, these methods may not be sufficiently developed for some domains, especially considering that new domains are constantly emerging, e.g., cloud hosting, IoT, etc. Besides, having help from the modeling language has advantages, as the place inside the model where the discovered elements should be put is already determined.

The two characteristics of modeling languages – expressive power and discovery power – are not entirely independent. The degree of dependency is related to the way these terms are defined. Also, these characteristics are not absolute; it is not always possible to say that one language has more expressive or discovery power than another. One language can have more power than the other only with respect to some elements that need to be depicted or discovered. Thus, the choice of language depends very much on the purpose for which a model is to be built. Also, in some circumstances, several modeling languages can be used. For example, one language with an appropriate discovery power is used to get an overall picture, and another language with a proper expressive power is used to add details to the overall picture.

This paper aims to introduce the concept of discovery power and suggest a way of establishing the discovery power of an enterprise modeling language. Methodologically, this work belongs to the Design Science (DS) paradigm [6], as its final goal is to develop an artifact – an approach to evaluate the discovery power of enterprise modeling languages. Note, however, that the style of this paper is nearer to the essay style than to the DS papers styles. This corresponds to our primary goal for this paper – to introduce and justify a new concept. The essay style is not uncommon for such a goal; for example, Michael Polanyi uses it to introduce the tacit dimension [7].

The rest of the paper is structured in the following manner. In Sect. 2, we analyze the already existing concept of expressive power. In Sect. 3, we introduce the concept of discovery power. In Sect. 4, we discuss the way of analyzing the discovery power of enterprise modeling languages. Section 5 contains concluding remarks and plans for the future.

2   Analyzing the Concept of Expressive Power

In this section, we will try to give a more exact definition of the concept of expressive power in relation to the chosen type of modeling languages, in our case, enterprise modeling languages, and chosen usage of the models, in our case, decision-making by human beings. The general notion of whether some pattern of reality can or cannot be expressed in the language does not give us much room for comparing languages. For example, most enterprise modeling languages have the concept of the association relation, with the help of which one can depict any relation between two concepts by adequately setting a label on the association. We consider that if one language uses a specific relation between two concepts, and the second one employs a generic relation, like an association, to depict the same kind of relations, the expressive power of these languages is different. More precisely, the first language has a higher expressive power with respect to the specific type of relations. The second language just "codes" the relation using more generic means.

To illustrate our way of thinking, below, we will present a pattern taken from [8], and present it in three different enterprise modeling languages. We do this exercise twice, first using abstract labels and second using labels that explain the elements' meaning. The three languages we use are ArchiMate [9], IDEF0 [10], and Fractal Enterprise Model (FEM) [11, 12][1]. The models with abstract labels are presented in Fig. 1a, 1b, and 2. Below, we present some explanations for those unfamiliar with these languages.

In the ArchiMate model, all elements, except Y, are from the technology layer:

- X represents a facility, which is shown by the icon in the upper right corner.
- Y represents a role, which is shown by the icon in the upper right corner. The role can be assigned to an agent.

---

[1] The choice of languages is based on (1) all these techniques having a certain degree of discovery power; (2) we have experience in using them in practice and/or educational contexts. As far as FEM is concerned, this modeling technique is our invention.

- Z represents equipment, which is shown by the icon in the upper right corner.
- V represents an interface, which is shown by the icon in the upper right corner. The interface is part of the equipment, which is shown by a special type of relations with a diamond tail; the relation is marked as #3.
- W represents behavior – a technology service, which is shown by the icon in the upper right corner.
- A, B, and C represent materials, which is shown by the icon in the upper right corner.
- The relation #1, represented by an arrow with a round tail, shows the assignment. There are three assignments in the model. Equipment Z is assigned to facility X, which means it is placed inside the facility. Service W is assigned to equipment Z, which means that equipment Z is used in service W. Role Y is assigned to facility X, which means that an agent that fulfills the role operates everything inside the facility.
- The relation between the interface and the role, marked by #2, is a serving relation; it means that role Y operates equipment Z via interface V.
- The relations #4 and #5 are access relations. The relations marked as #4, with a dashed line and arrows on both ends, are of type *read/write*, which means that service W both investigates materials A and B and changes them. The relation marked as #5 is of type *write*, which means that W changes C.

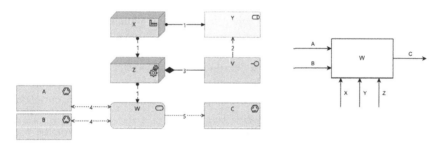

Fig. 1. Anonymous model. (a) Left - a model in ArchiMate. (b) Right - the same model in IDEF0.

In the IDEF0 model of Fig. 1b, a rectangle represents a function; it can be a business or a technological function. Arrows coming from the left represent the inputs of the function, and arrows coming out on the right represent the outputs of the function. Arrows coming to the bottom represent mechanisms used to transform inputs into outputs; it can be people, equipment, etc. Arrows coming to the top represent control mechanisms that steer the function execution; there is none in Fig. 1b. The connection between the functions is presented as output from one function coming as input, mechanism, or control to another function. Some arrows can come outside the given organization, and some outputs can go outside the given organization. The model in Fig. 1b has only one functional shape representing function W that transforms inputs A and B into output C, using X, Y, and Z as mechanisms. Note that element V from the ArchiMate model has no representation in this IDEF0 model.

In the FEM model of Fig. 2, an oval represents a process – a repetitive behavior; a rectangle represents an asset – a set of things or actors that can be used in or managed by a process. An arrow with a solid line represents the *used-in* relation between an asset

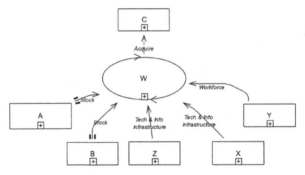

Fig. 2. The same model in FEM (anonymous)

and a process; each arrow is provided with one or several labels from a standardized set of 8 labels. An arrow with a dashed line represents the *managed-by* relation between the asset and the process; each arrow is provided with one or several labels from the standardized set of three labels – *Acquire, Maintain,* and *Retire.* The first label means that new elements are added to the asset, the second label means that some elements are changed to restore their working conditions, and the third label means that the elements are removed from the set.

The label *stock* has a special meaning; it shows that some of the elements of the asset are consumed in each successful run of the process (a run is one cycle of repetitive behavior represented by a process). The special meaning of *stock* is also represented by the corresponding arrow's special tale (starting point). The *stock* label can be assigned to an arrow alone or accompanied by another label. When alone, it represents some consumables – parts of the assembly, reserve parts, etc. This label roughly corresponds to the input concept of IDEF0 (see Fig. 1b).

Comparing the anonymous models, we can see that some aspects of the model are given more precisely in one model than in the others. For example, we can see that X is a facility, Y is a role, and Z is equipment in ArchiMate. In IDEF0, X, Y, and Z are mechanisms without any precision of what kind. FEM takes an intermediate position between the other two. X and Z serve as technical and info infrastructure; Y is a workforce, i.e., people employed by the given organization. Relations #4 and #5 in ArchiMate do not explain what for A, B, and C are used. In IDEF0, A and B are inputs, and C is an output. The same is expressed by the *Stock* relation for A and B, and *Acquire* relation for C in FEM. The latter means that process W adds new elements to C.

Now, let us have a look at the same models but with properly set labels, which are represented in Fig. 3a, 3b, and 4. The model in Fig. 3a was taken from [8] (View 30) and slightly adjusted by setting labels on the access relations. With the labels, the models could be equally understandable for business people, except that some facts are not represented in all of them; for example, the interface is not presented in the IDEF0 and FEM models. Also, the equipment being inside the factory is not represented in IDEF0 and FEM, but it could be easily understood by a business person investigating the model based on common sense.

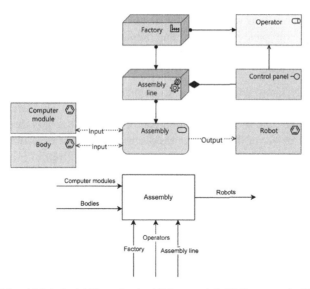

Fig. 3. Models with labels. (a) Top - the ArchiMate model. (b) Bottom - the IDEF0 model.

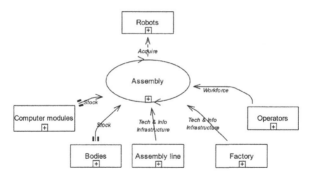

Fig. 4. The same model in FEM (with labels).

Going back to the concept of the expressive power of enterprise modeling languages, we give two different definitions of the concept:

1. **Absolute expressive power** is defined via negation. It concerns whether some part of reality can be expressed in a given language. If it cannot be expressed, we say that the given language **does not have** the expressive power to depict this part of reality. According to this definition, a language where most relations are depicted as associations, as in UML class diagrams, has quite good expressive power.

2. **Relative expressive power** for comparing languages that have the absolute expressive power to depict a specific part of reality. Suppose some part of reality is expressed by specific means in one language and by more generic means in another. In that case, the first language has a **greater expressive power** than the second one with respect to this part of reality. A good way to discover the difference is to compare

anonymized models, as was done in the first exercise in this section. IDEF0 and FEM have a better expressive power regarding output/input relations than ArchiMate. The latter uses more generic means – *access relation,* while the other two use specific means for output/input.

If we already know what we need to depict, the first definition can be used for choosing the language, and the second can be totally ignored. If, however, we need to discover and depict, the second definition can be important as it is directly connected to the discovery power of the language, as discussed in the next section. Note that the definition of expressive power in programming languages given in [4] corresponds to our definition of relative expressive power.

3 Introducing the Concept of Discovery Power

To introduce the concept of discovery power, we need to discuss the context in which the model is being built and used. We will use an OODA loop as suggested by Boyd [13], which is depicted in Fig. 5, though this sketch was meant for a different situation than ours[2]. The central point of the OODA loop is *Orient* – an activity that allows one to get a clear view of the situation, which is then used to generate a hypothesis for action (*Decide*). The orientation in the *Orient* phase is done based on the information from the *Observe* phase obtained under the guidance and control from the *Orient* phase.

The OODA loop is based on managing implicit or tacit knowledge, in terms of Michael Polanyi [7]. This relates to Boyd's military profession, dog pilot, and the need to make and change decisions quickly. Therefore, the model of the situation produced by orientation and used for decision-making is made on the tacit, not explicit, level. For building this tacit model, the actor (usually one person) uses his/her experience and so-called his/her mental (general model) of reality. These components also guide the observation activity.

A situation where an enterprise model is built and used is different, as it has an explicit component in both building the model and gathering data for building it; the latter is equivalent to the *Observe* phase. Applying the OODA cycle in this situation requires an adaptation of the diagram presented in Fig. 5. An explicit model is provided by the *Orient* phase to the *Decide* phase (*Feed forward* in Fig. 5). Moreover, the *Orient* phase should provide not only implicit but also explicit guidance to the *Observe* phase. This is in line with other works that adapt the OODA cycle for business analysis; see, for example, the work of Patrick Hoverstadt [14], who adapted the OODA cycle for agile strategy development and implementation.

In this paper, we are primarily interested in two phases *Observe* and *Orient*. Feed forward from the *Observe* phase to the *Orient* phase is information based on which an enterprise model is being built. For our case, these two phases and their connection are presented in Fig. 6. Feed forward from *Orient* to *Decide* is an enterprise model based on which a decision on actions is taken. In general, the model should include

---

[2] The choice of the OODA cycle for describing the context of building models is based on it being in correspondence with our experience. The choice does not exclude the application of other approaches, but this issue is outside the scope of this paper.

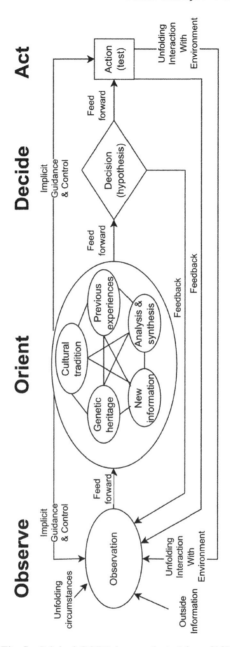

Fig. 5. Original OODA loop, adapted from [13].

information about the environment of the enterprise in focus, e.g., competitors, and about the enterprise itself, e.g., its capabilities. The information needed to build the model can be obtained from different sources, including documents describing the environment or the organization itself, interviews with stakeholders, facilitating workshops with them, and actual observations of what is happening outside or inside the organization.

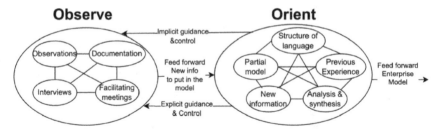

Fig. 6. Adaptation of OODA cycle for a case when orient should produce an explicit model (only two phases presented)

Gathering new information in the *Observe* phase is guided and controlled partly implicitly (as in Fig. 5) and partly explicitly. Explicit guidance and control can be in the form of questions for interviews, instructions on what specific information is missing and needs to be obtained, etc. This control is partly defined by the experience and background of the modelers, which is depicted in Fig. 5 as *Previous experience, Cultural Heritage* and *Genetic Heritage*. The other part is provided by the structure of the modeling language that is used to build the model. This structure defines which entities and relations should be found in the environment and organization. For example, based on this structure, specific interview questions can be asked, or gaps in the model being built initiate looking for certain kinds of information in the documents.

We consider that the chosen language has enough absolute expressive power for the current task. The need to have better relative expressive power depends on the concrete situation. For example, if the modeling team has experience in modeling a similar organization, then the guidance for *Observe* and building the model can be based on the experience. Another example is when the language is quite general, but there exists additional material on how to use it in certain situations, e.g., a set of patterns that can be looked for, which are expressed in the language. In a situation where the domain to which the targeted organization belongs is new for the modeling team, and there are few easy-to-use guiding materials, the structure of the modeling language could help. This can be true if the language has specific means for expressing certain important ideas, i.e., it has a better relative expressive power than other possible languages. These specific means can provide explicit guidance and control for gathering information and building the model.

Note that the OODA loop does not imply that its four phases are done consequently; they all happen simultaneously, and there is tight cooperation between them. It means that building an enterprise model starts as soon as some data has been obtained, and new guidance is produced to get information to continue building the model and filling gaps discovered in it. Based on this deliberation, we can define the concept of *Discovery power* of an enterprise modeling language as.

"Degree of help provided by the structure of enterprise modeling language to expand a partly built model or fill gaps in it".

Under the structure here, we mean not only syntax but a combination of syntax, semantics, and pragmatics of the language that facilitates looking for missing information. This help consists of explicit guidance and control provided by the *Orient* phase to the *Observe* phase. Consider an example: suppose we use IDEF0 as a modeling language and already have a functional element F with an output O. The relevant guidance for the *Observe* phase is to find another functional element for which O serves as an *Input*, *Control*, or *Mechanism*. There are two options: (1) it already exists in the model, (2) it does not exist in the model. In case (1), a connection between two functional elements of the type *output-input*, *output-mechanism*, or *output-control* is added. In case (2), a new element and a new connection are added to the model. In both cases, the model is extended, or some gap is filled. This example shows that IDEF0 has a *Discovery power* of a specific type – finding new functional elements connected to the already known functional elements based on *output-input*, *output-mechanism*, or *output-control* relations between the functional elements.

As we can see from the example, the discovery power is connected to specific means to express specific ideas, e.g., input, output, mechanism and control. If all relations were presented as an association or access (as in ArchiMate), the discovery power to add new elements to the model would have been lost, and the modelers would be left to rely on their experience or additional materials to find new functional elements.

The original OODA cycle has only implicit guidance and control from the *Orient* to *Observe* phase. This is consistent with a military situation, especially in a dogfight, when there is no time for explicit control. One of the differences between Fig. 5 and our adaptation in Fig. 6 consists of feedback from *Orient* to *Observe* on the tacit (implicit) level in Fig. 5 is complemented by the feedback on the explicit level. However, this change does not imply that the *Orient* phase does not have constraints in the form of limitations on the resources, including time available for finishing the task. The time to build the model in a practical project is always limited, as well as, for example, the availability of stakeholders to answer questions. Therefore, additional means provided by the structure of the language for getting information could be of value unless the team has other means that provide this information quicker. In case of a modeling team lacking experience in the domain, the discovery power of the modeling language can help in completing the modeling project with constraints on resources, including time, and producing a model of a good enough quality.

As follows from the deliberation above, the discovery power of a language lies in specific means to express some ideas. The more specific these means are, the more discovery power the language has with respect to the ideas expressed by these means. Actually, any language that can be used for enterprise modeling has some specific means for expressing some specific ideas. Also, there are some specific means that many languages share. For example, a specialization relation, which exists in many modeling languages, can be used to ask a specific question after some conceptual element was put in the partially built model, e.g., a customer: "Do you have different kinds of customers?" This question can provide explicit guidance/control to the *Observe* phase.

Despite similarities between enterprise modeling languages, some expressive means are specific to a specific language. For example, the ArchiMate's specific means are quite different from those of IDEF0 and FEM, as could be seen from the discussion in Sect. 2. Specific means in IDEF0 and FEM are more in line with each other; see [15] that compares these languages. The specific means for expressing the ideas determine the discovery power of the language. As they are different for different languages, the investigation of their discovery power needs to be done separately for each language.

Using an adapted OODA cycle in the deliberations above is directly connected to the fact that our definition of *discovery power* concerns the help a modeling language provides for building so-called as-is models. This is the primary usage envisioned for the new concept. This said, nothing prevents using the concept in other situations, for example, if one wants to create a model for a new business, e.g., a start-up. However, this concept is too general to be useful for analyzing as-is models to find places for intervention, though it can be partly helpful in deciding how a to-be model should look. The usage of the concept of discovery power in contexts other than building as-is models is outside the scope of the current paper.

4 Formal Discovery Rules and Their Limitations

As was defined in the previous section, the discovery power of a language can be expressed by the level of explicit control the language structure can provide for extending a partially built model or filling gaps in it. The idea can be formalized as a set of *discovery rules*, each of which has two parts: (1) a *query pattern* that should match a small fragment of an already built model, and (2) an *extended pattern* that includes new elements to be found. Figure 7 presents an example of such a rule for ArchiMate.

In this example, the left part shows the *query pattern* – a service with an assigned actor and an application component that supports the service. The right part shows the *extended pattern* that includes an application interface the actor uses to operate the application component. Thus, a new element, highlighted with the rose (gray in the B&W print) background color, should be added to the model and connected to the already existing elements by the composition relation (to the application component) and the serving relation (to the business actor). Another example of the same sort is presented in Fig. 8. It also concerns finding an application interface that the actor uses for invoking a particular application service.

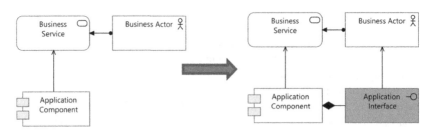

Fig. 7. A discovery rule for ArchiMate: left – query pattern; right – extended pattern

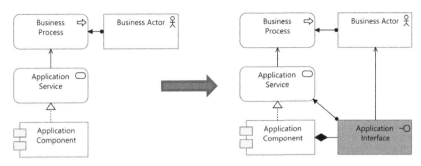

Fig. 8. Another rule for ArchiMate: left – query pattern; right – extended pattern

In Fig. 9, we present an example of a discovery rule for IDEF0. Suppose the output of a functional element has been established. In that case, the next step is to find where it goes, thus finding another functional element that consumes the output as input, control, or mechanism.

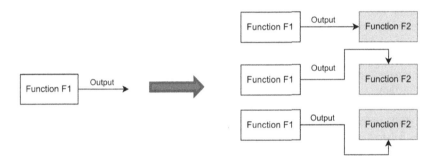

Fig. 9. A discovery rule for IDEF0: left – query pattern; right – extended pattern

In Fig. 10, we present an example of a discovery rule for FEM of a different nature. If the process concerns hiring new staff members, there should be some attraction for the candidates to join. It can be a good salary, excellent working environment, prospects for career development, etc.

The examples of rules presented above look quite formal; they need to be translated in a more "human form" dependent on what sources will be used to find missing information. For example, suppose we use interviews to find missing information when the rule in Fig. 7 is applied. In that case, we can ask: "What kind of interface does the business actor have to access the application component when he/she is using it to complete activities in the business service?" For the rule in Fig. 8, this question can be specified more precisely: "Which interface is used to invoke the application service that supports the business process?" This kind of questions may not be answered satisfactorily. The interviewer may need to reformulate it differently, e.g., "Which categories of users does the access control system define for the application component?", and then try to find out to which category the business actor belongs.

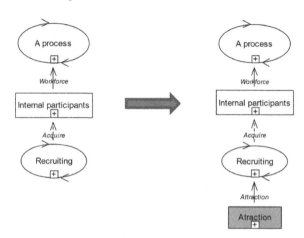

Fig. 10. A discovery rule for FEM: left - query pattern; right – extended pattern

Suppose we use observations for finding missing information, and we want to follow the rule in Fig. 9. In that case, we need to understand where the output of *F1* is going, and after the component *F2* is found, try to understand what this output is used for: as an input, mechanism, or control. Suppose we use documents to find the missing information, and we want to follow the rule in Fig. 10. In that case, we can investigate the company's advertisement material to see what they offer to the potential candidates.

The above examples from three different enterprise modeling languages show that it is possible to define the rules of discovery formally. However, their application requires some skills and experience in processing sources of information. An experienced modeler may not need the formal rules to use the discovery power of the language. This is especially true for a language with a limited number of ideas that can be expressed by special means, as in IDEF0. If the number of special means is great and/or the modeler is less experienced, having formal rules of the type presented in Fig. 7, 8, 9 and 10 makes sense. An example of a language with many kinds of special means is ArchiMate. It has many types of concepts, and some of them are repeated on different levels. In addition, there are several ways of connecting them with relations, e.g., realization, serving, access, etc. So, defining some formal discovery rules for ArchiMate makes sense even for more experienced modelers, especially if they are new to the language.

Having formal rules of the type, as in Fig. 7, 8, 9 and 10, is insufficient to provide explicit guidance and control going from the *Orient* to *Observe* phase. They need to be converted to more exact instructions, like what questions to ask, what to observe, what documents to look at, and for what. This can be left to the modeler to do, or we need to add some guidelines on how to find missing information to the formal rules. The latter can be quite handy for less experienced modelers. An example of converting a kind of discovery rules for FEM in interview questions is presented in [16].

The formal rules could also be used to partly automate building the models. One can envision an algorithm that scans a partly built model against the formal rules and suggests which elements must be found. The modeler then uses available sources of information to find these elements and add them to the model, after which the scan is repeated. The cycle stops when the algorithm can no longer find which new elements could be added.

5 Concluding Remarks and Plans for the Future

As stated in the Introduction, this paper aims to introduce a new concept – the discovery power of enterprise modeling languages and clarify its relation to the well-known concept of the expressive power of a language. The primary motivation behind introducing the new concept is that something is missing when the decision is made on which enterprise modeling language(s) to use in a particular modeling project. During the writing of this article, an additional goal emerged - to present some ideas on how the discovery power of an enterprise modeling language can be established.

In Sect. 3, we related the discovery power to the help the structure of language could provide in building an enterprise model. We also connected it to the relative definition of expressive power. The importance of discovery power depends on the context of language usage. When the organization's activities are well-known to the modeling team, having satisfactory expressive power is enough for choosing the language. However, if the domain is new for the team, and there are limitations on the resources available, e.g., time to build a model, help from the structure of a modeling language can be important when choosing a language.

In Sect. 4, we suggested a possible structure of formal rules that describe the discovery power of an enterprise modeling language. Such a rule consists of two parts: (1) a query pattern and (2) an extended pattern, which shows what needs to be found. The approach was illustrated by examples of rules for three enterprise modeling languages, ArchiMate, IDEF0, and FEM. This part is a transition from introducing the concept to developing an artifact (from the DS point of view) - an approach for evaluating the discovery power of enterprise modeling languages.

The plans for the near future include defining formal discovery rules for the three enterprise modeling languages used for discussions in this paper. Completing this exercise will give us more information on how the rules should be structured and how to evaluate the discovery power of enterprise modeling languages.

Acknowledgment. The Estonian Research Council (grant PRG1226) partly supported the first author's work. The authors are thankful to Paul Johannesson, who suggested that there is a coupling between the expressive and discovery power. The authors are also grateful to the anonymous reviewers whose comments helped improve the text.

References

1. Felleisen, M.: On the expressive power of programming languages. Sci. Comput. Program. **17**, 35–75 (1991)
2. Wikipedia: Expressive power (computer science). https://en.wikipedia.org/wiki/Expressive_power_(computer_science)

3. Van der Aalst, W.M., ter Hofstede, A.H.: On the expressive power of (petri-net-based) work-flow languages. In: Proceedings of the Fourth Workshop on the Practical Use of Coloured Petri Nets and CPN Tools (CPN 2002), vol. 560, pp. 1–20 (2002)

4. Wilson, L.B., Clark, R.G.: Comparative Programming Languages. Pearson Education, Upper Saddle River (2001)

5. Fowler, M.: Analysis Patterns: Reusable Object Models. Addison-Wesley Professional, Reading (2015)

6. Hevner, A., March, S.T., Park, J.: Design science in information systems research. MIS Q. **28**(1), 75–105 (2004)

7. Polanyi, M.: The structure of consciousness. Brain **LXXXVIII**, 799–810 (1965)

8. Wierda, G.: Mastering Archimate Edition 3.1. P&A (2022)

9. The Open Group: ArchiMate® 3.2 Specification. In: The Open Group. https://publications.opengroup.org/standards/archimate/specifications/c226. Accessed 2022

10. NIST: Integration definition for function modeling (IDEF0), Draft Federal Information Processing Standards, Publication 183. In: IDEF (1993). https://www.idef.com/idefo-function_modeling_method/. Accessed 1993

11. Bider, I., Perjons, E., Elias, M., Johannesson, P.: A fractal enterprise model and its application for business development. SoSyM **16**(3), 663–689 (2017)

12. Bider, I., Perjons, E., Klyukina, V.: Tool support for fractal enterprise modeling. In: Karagiannis, D., Lee, M., Hinkelmann, K., Utz, W. (eds.) Domain-Specific Conceptual Modeling, pp. 205–229. Springer, Cham (2022) https://doi.org/10.1007/978-3-030-93547-4_10

13. Boyd, J.: The essence of winning and losing. Unpublished Lecture Notes **12**(23), 123–125. http://www.expertsecho.com/johnboyd/johnboyd_docs/Essence_of_Winning_and_Losing.pdf. Accessed Aug 2010

14. Hoverstadt, P., Loh, L.: Patterns of Strategy. Taylor & Francis, New York (2017)

15. Bider, I., Perjons, E., Johanneson, P.: Using ontologies for comparing modeling techniques: experience report. In: Guizzardi, G., Gailly, F., Suzana Pitangueira Maciel, R. (eds.) ER 2019. LNCS, vol. 11787, pp. 180–190. Springer, Cham (2019). https://doi.org/10.1007/978-3-030-34146-6_16

16. Leego, S., Bider, I.: Improving IT governance, security and privacy using fractal enterprise modeling: a case of a highly regulated company. In: Hinkelmann, K., López-Pellicer, F.J., Polini, A. (eds.) BIR 2023. LNBIP, vol. 493, pp. 199–213. Springer, Cham (2023). https://doi.org/10.1007/978-3-031-43126-5_15

Towards a Multidimensional View
on Traceability in IT

Anna De Vos$^{(\boxtimes)}$ ⓘ and Jan Verelst

University of Antwerp, Antwerp, Belgium
annadevos2000@gmail.com

Abstract. Traceability is a central concept in the domain of Enterprise Engineering. Indeed, the controlled transformation of the more business-oriented requirements layers to designs and runtime code has been studied over the years in domains such as IT Governance, Enterprise Architecture, and Software Development. However, traceability on the entire flow from business to IT is often lacking in complex projects in industry, thereby hampering the agility, productivity, and resilience of organizations in the digital era. Consequentially, organizations often fail to realize IT business value. Therefore, we investigate how the traceability issue in IT can be defined, and to what extent traceability issues still exist in practice based on 28 interviews with 16 interviewees from various organizations, differing in industry, size, and geographical location. Results indicate that opinions on the value and importance of traceability vary greatly, along with the views on how realistic it is to establish traceability in practice. Also, available theories and frameworks do not seem to be applied in many cases, even though they are not completely unknown to the interviewees. Clearly, there is a gap between theory and practice regarding traceability. The reasons for this are not entirely clear from this research. However, we call for new, holistic, and integrated research on traceability across multiple domains, highlighting the multidimensionality of the traceability issue in IT, and fostered in the Enterprise Engineering community.

Keywords: Traceability · Enterprise Architecture · Governance · Traceability

1 Introduction

So far, the 21st century has been marked by a rapidly changing environment with unprecedented innovation velocity. Customer needs and preferences continuously change, and the role of IT is shifting from supporting business processes to a primary driver of business value. In this rapidly changing and complex environment, agility is of the utmost importance for organizations [1]. Thus, an organization's structure, including its business processes and information systems, must be adapted accordingly to maintain and support a competitive advantage [2].

Despite numerous innovations in recent years, productivity seems to lag, as initially described by the Solow Paradox [3, 5]. Many years later, the Solow Paradox seems to be applicable again. In spite of the enormous investments in IT, companies often do not realize their full potential as they fail to restructure their business accordingly [6, 6] and fail to exploit the advantages of IT investments because of a misalignment between business and IT [7, 8]. Indeed, changing requirements within an organization should be translated into changes in its business processes and the IT landscape. A lack of traceability could harm the organization's agility capability and, therefore, contribute to the productivity paradox [9].

In this paper, we argue that traceability should be considered across multiple domains, thereby highlighting the need for a multidimensional approach to traceability.

This paper is structured as follows. In Sect. 2, the research methodology is discussed. Thereafter, Sect. 3 introduces traceability and discusses the traceability issue within three domains of interest: IT Governance, Enterprise Architecture, and Software Development. In Sect. 4, the results from our empirical research into traceability in practice are presented. Finally, in Sect. 5, we discuss the findings and offer our conclusions.

2 Research Questions and Methodology

2.1 Research Questions

The aim of this study is to understand the nature and causes of the traceability issue in IT. Therefore, different domains and perspectives that could explain this phenomenon, described in the literature, are studied. Furthermore, different experts and companies are interviewed to gather insights from practice. Based on the research objective, a main research question is identified: "What causes a lack of traceability within an organization's IT environment?". This research question is split into multiple sub-questions:

- How can the traceability issue in IT be defined, and what are its characteristics?
- What causes a lack of traceability in the domains of software development, Enterprise Architecture, and IT governance?
- To what extent is there a lack of traceability in IT in practice?
- What challenges are organizations currently facing in relation to traceability in IT?

2.2 Research Methodology

This empirical research is conducted using an explorative research design, and more specifically interviews. The choice of such a design rests on the inherent nature of IS research to study information systems within their real-life settings and fields of application [10]. This critical feature perfectly matches the intent of this research since the research questions focus on the traceability issue of an organization's IT environment [11, 12]. Moreover, conducting multiple interviews with multiple organizations and experts results in a higher external validity and is better suited for theory building.

Different research design properties have been evaluated to enhance the quality of the research. The table below gives an overview of the various properties of the research design and the initiatives undertaken to strengthen them (Table 1).

Table 1. Research design properties.

Property	Research design
External validity	To increase the generalizability of the research, data source triangulation in the form of multiple semi-structured interviews [13], and method triangulation in the form of semi-structured interviews triangulated by desk research is used
Internal validity	To increase the construct validity of the research, each interviewee is asked to review the interview outcomes [14]. It is essential to note that the goal is to correct false interpretations, not to change the research interpretations or outcomes [15]. Moreover, prolonged engagement and thick description strategies are used to strengthen the trust relationships with the interviewees, resulting in more and richer data [16]
Reliability	To strengthen the reliability of this research, a standardized interview guide is determined [14]. In addition, member checks, and more precisely between different interviewees, are performed to enhance the reliability of the research [16]

For the selection of cases, purposeful sampling is used to target the companies and experts with the most experience and know-how about the field of research [17]. This sampling technique ensures that the necessary interviewees are in the sample, which is not the case when using a random sampling strategy. A well-known point of criticism is related to the number of interviews to conduct. On the one hand, it is often argued that a too-low number of instances constricts the validity of the research [11]. On the other hand, conducting too many interviews minimizes incremental learning. Therefore, the theoretical saturation point is used to determine the number of interviews.

The data in this research is gathered using desk research and semi-structured interviews. Desk research is used in preparation for the interviews and to evaluate the interview outcomes. Interviews are suited to study traceability because of the importance of and implications on everyday real life [18]. A drawback of this data collection method is the dependency on the knowledgeableness of the interviewees [18]. Therefore, to strengthen the argument made earlier, purposeful sampling is used. This way, the quality of the interview answers and expertise of the interviewees can be somewhat guaranteed. Table 2 gives an overview of the interviews. In total, 28 interviews with 16 interviewees have been conducted. The interviewees are knowledgeable in different domains, mainly focusing on business & IT management, Enterprise Architecture, and software development.

Table 2. Interview overview.

Type	# interviewees	Industry	Country (HQ)	Size (FTE)
Operational organizations				
Less mature organization in terms of EA	5	Industrial equipment	Sweden	>30.000
Mature organizations in terms of EA	2	Retail	Belgium	>30.000
Expert interviews				
Consultancy practitioners company A	2	Consultancy	Belgium	<500
Consultancy practitioner company B	1	Consultancy	Belgium	<100
Consultancy practitioners company C	4	Consultancy	Belgium	<500
Industry & Academic expert	2	Energy	France	>90.000

3 Background

3.1 The Origin of Traceability Research

Traceability in IT was initially addressed within the software development domain. Multiple definitions of traceability exist within this domain. The ISO/IEC/IEEE International Standard [19] defines traceability as "The degree to which a relationship can be established between two or more products of the development process, especially products having a predecessor-successor or master-subordinate relationship to one another.". Multiple authors have also addressed the difficulty of providing traceability. For example, Mäder & Gotel [20] highlight cost as an essential factor in realizing traceability in IT. The authors give two reasons for the high cost of providing traceability: the number of artifacts and maintaining their relations when change occurs.

Despite the ubiquitousness of traceability research within the software domain and the growing importance of traceability between multiple information systems, research [20, 21] often merely focuses on traceability links between requirements or models of one information system. Nevertheless, the traceability issues are not limited to the software domain. Indeed, traceability research has been conducted on multiple topics, such as traceability between different modeling languages, traceability of design choices, and traceability within project and change management. This diversity of traceability research topics highlights the complexity and versatility of the traceability issue in IT. Therefore, to fully understand this issue, traceability should be discussed across multiple domains. To this extent, the following section reflects on traceability within the domains of IT governance, Enterprise Architecture (EA), and software development.

3.2 IT Governance and Traceability

Governance of IT emerged as an answer to the increasing importance of IT. Over the years, the understanding that IT cannot be solely responsible for creating IT-enabled business value resulted in the alignment between business and IT as one of the main goals of IT governance [22, 23]. Moreover, multiple studies state that IT governance contributes to realizing IT business value [6, 22, 24, 25]. More specifically, it is argued that a lack of good IT Governance results in a lack of alignment and consequentially, a lack of IT business value creation and protection [19, 23].

To guide organizations in the effective governance of their IT, the Information Systems Audit and Control Association (ISACA) developed the Control Objectives for Information Technologies (COBIT) framework [26]. COBIT identifies six Enterprise Governance of IT (EGIT) components and 40 governance and management objectives, which are instantiated based on the unique situation and environment of an organization. When an EGIT system is not effective, business and IT alignment will be hampered, traceability between business and IT requirements might be missing, and the creation and protection of IT business value cannot be ensured [22, 26].

The link between IT governance and traceability can be illustrated using an example. Organizations typically have multiple projects running at the same time. Therefore, proper project and program management are essential to provide an overview of the different projects and to improve alignment between the different artifacts of those projects [27]. A lack of alignment between different (IT) projects and their artifacts leads to multiple problems. Op 't Land et al. list, among others, the following shortcomings: realized solutions overlap or are incomplete, realized solutions are incompatible, and a lack of interoperability and consistency [28]. The management objective 'Managed Portfolio' (APO05) of COBIT deals with this issue [26]. The first activity in the third process step of this objective deals with the elimination of duplication among programs. To do so, projects in the portfolio are traced back to the IT strategy. This way, when organizations can trace back multiple projects to the same IT requirement, duplications can be identified and eliminated. Thus, traceability is needed to ensure alignment between business and IT, and consequentially ensure the creation of IT business value.

3.3 Enterprise Architecture and Traceability

EA allows managing the complexity of multiple processes and information systems and provides a holistic perspective on organizations, capturing organizational structures, business processes, applications, and IT infrastructure [29, 30]. Thus, EA should allow for traceability between the different domains in an organization [31]. Nevertheless, there are some considerable traceability issues within the domain of EA.

A first traceability issue is that of frameworks, methods, and modeling languages being of a descriptive nature, thereby insufficiently dealing with traceability from a theoretical perspective. Zachman [33] is a product-based descriptive framework, while TOGAF's ADM [32] is a prescriptive but process-based framework, with both of them lacking prescriptive guidelines on traceability of products. Furthermore, ArchiMate [34] is a modeling language, and therefore also non-prescriptive. Additionally, Zachman and ArchiMate are both composed of multiple layers and descriptions or aspects, but both approaches struggle with the link between different layers. Zachman recognizes that subsequent layers do not merely present "another level of detail" but are different in nature [33]. Likewise, arrows in ArchiMate are drawn manually. Thus, there is no systematic mapping from one layer to another [30].

The scope of EA approaches presents another traceability issue. First of all, the scope of EA is to provide a holistic view of the entire organization, yet traceability to the code is lacking. For example, ArchiMate does not possess a code layer [35]. Consequentially, there is no link (not even a manual one) from the EA models to the final code. Multiple research papers address this issue regarding software development artifacts and code (see e.g. Antoniol et al. [36]). This is important as, considering the research of Mäder & Gotel among others, the high cost related to providing traceability, programmers might directly modify the code without adjustments to the respective software architecture artifacts [20]. In addition, Murta et al. argue that a lack of a systematic and automatic mapping of documents and models to respective coding results in a lack of traceability [37]. This reasoning can easily be extended to the domain of EA; since traceability from software models to code is already a challenge, extending that traceability towards (higher-level) EA models is probably an even bigger challenge.

Second, EA starts from the strategic decisions made in organizations. More specifically, when strategic decisions are made, the organization might need to be restructured (i.e., the architecture will change) [38]. In his paper titled Strategy and Architecture – Reconciling Worldviews, van Gils identifies some causes of the existing tensions between strategists and architects: overlapping domains, different language, and different worldviews [38]. Interestingly, he states that the tension between strategists and architects is especially present in organizations where EA is regarded as pure IT. This tension between strategists and architects hinders traceability from the strategy to EA.

A third traceability issue in the domain of EA is the existence of a heterogeneous landscape of modeling languages. Multiple modeling languages exist to model (parts of) an enterprise, such as BPMN and UML. This heterogeneous landscape of modeling languages results in integration and alignment issues between models from different languages [39]. Consequentially, traceability between models from a different modeling language needs to be improved. Multiple papers have been written on the lack of traceability between these different models and levels within the organizations [30, 40].

A last traceability perspective states that traceability can be strengthened by documenting requirements and the reasoning behind certain design decisions. Plataniotis et al. suggest using requirements in the gap analysis as a bridge between two states, allowing alignment between stakeholder requirements and IS development outputs [42]. Design rationale is focused on the reason for certain design decisions. Interestingly, Tang et al. state that, in practice, there is no systematic documentation of the justification of decisions [43]. This especially becomes a problem when architects who were not included in the development phase are responsible for the maintenance of systems.

3.4 Software Development and Traceability

Considering the previously introduced software development domain, two traceability topics are discussed in more detail: Combinatorial Effects (CEs) and Model-Driven Engineering (MDE).

The CEs issue finds its origin in the degradation of software architectures over time, resulting in unmanageable, complex information systems that are costly to maintain and critical information consistently out-of-date or just plain wrong [44]. This degradation process is described by Lehman's Law of Increasing Complexity, which is formulated as follows: "As an evolving program is continuously changed, its complexity, reflecting deteriorating structure, increases unless work is done to maintain it or reduce it" [47, p. 216]. Closely related to this law, Combinatorial Effects (CEs) occur when a change impact to a software architecture depends on the size of a software system, which means that the effort needed to apply a change to an information system increases over time, similar to what Lehman's Law predicts [45]. To avoid such CEs, Mannaert et al. proposed their Normalized Systems Theory (NST) which focuses on designing evolvable and modular software systems and EA [45, 47, 48]. Hereby, the authors link the software development domain to the traceability issue in IT by highlighting the need to systematically apply software design theorems, as a lack of such an approach will inevitably lead to increasingly complex systems, hampering traceability over time.

Since EA takes a more holistic view of the enterprise than software, this domain is specifically interesting regarding traceability. Van Nuffel et al. argue that CEs are not limited to software but are also present in EA: "If a change in a certain model affects other models it is combined with, a combinatorial effect occurs." [49, p. 243].

Traceability in terms of code generation based on Model-Driven Engineering (MDE) refers to traceability between models that serve as primary artifacts for software development. Galvao & Goknil argue that MDE must consider traceability to identify relationships and dependencies between software artifacts [49]. Moreover, the authors identify multiple traceability issues, such as metamodels falling short of enabling traceability, heterogeneity of models making it difficult to provide fine-grained trace links, and the automatic updating of trace links which are not sufficiently considered.

4   Traceability in Practice

The interviews confirmed that, indeed, the traceability issue in IT is a multifaceted and complex issue that exists on the entire flow from business to IT. In what follows, the most important results are discussed per domain of interest.

4.1   IT Governance

First of all, there is consensus among the participants on the necessity of support for EA at the top (i.e., strategy/board level). For example, van Gils claims that the demand for traceability should come from the top because, without traceability, strategists cannot make well-informed decisions [50]. Nevertheless, there is a lack of awareness of the importance and value of traceability in practice. Multiple interviewees mention that traceability is not talked about in organizations. This may be related to the limitation of research to the acknowledgment and understanding of the value of IT, which does not discuss the acknowledgment and understanding of the value of traceability [7, 26].

Second, multiple interviewees claim that EA is positioned under IT in most organizations. Consequently, architects are involved too late in the decision-making process, which, according to the experts, hinders traceability. Indeed, when EA is regarded as pure IT, the tension between strategists and architects is typically high [50]. This is especially problematic when taking into account the chain of decision-making. If business and IT fail to understand each other (i.e., lack of alignment), it is challenging to trace decisions and artifacts on the flow from business to IT.

Third, the IT governance maturity of organizations is often questionable. For example, during the interviews, it became clear that most organizations do not perform a feedback loop after completing projects to check whether objectives have been reached.

Furthermore, multiple interviewees questioned the value of traceability. One interviewee states that even if there is traceability, IT teams can still develop the wrong things. However, if there is traceability on the entire flow from business to IT, and thus to the strategy, there is a guarantee that projects contribute to strategic objectives and therefore develop the right artefacts.

Finally, most interviewees agree that traceability between the (business) strategy and the architecture is a challenge, and therefore also between projects and strategy. Nevertheless, COBIT clearly states that IT business value cannot be ensured without traceability from projects to the strategy. Therefore, it is surprising that precisely this link between IT and strategy seems challenging in practice. In fact, alignment between business and IT, and thus traceability between the business strategy and IT, is the essence of IT governance [7, 26]. The tension between strategists and architects could explain why traceability between strategy and projects remains so difficult.

4.2 Enterprise Architecture

This section focuses on the EA implications and conclusions from the interviews.

First, all EA experts indicate that when communicating with business stakeholders ArchiMate models should not be used. Instead, some translation must happen to clarify EA options and implications for business stakeholders. When there is unclear and confusing communication with stakeholders, traceability is hindered as business stakeholders will not understand implications on lower levels within the organization. Thus, for communication purposes, tools like PowerPoint and Excel are used in practice. Moreover, in small and medium-sized enterprises, PowerPoint is still the primary tool for EA. This is not entirely unexpected given the smaller (IT) size of these organizations. However, the interviews also clarified that the knowledge on and understanding of the importance of IT traceability is often negligeable in these organizations.

Second, multiple experts argue that theoretical frameworks such as TOGAF should not be followed blindly. Using these frameworks does not necessarily lead to good results since they do not to specify the best option (i.e., Sect. 3.3; first EA perspective).

Third, many experts refer to the 'ivory tower' (i.e. a situation in which architects are no longer in contact with operational matters). Since good EA should allow for traceability, such an 'ivory tower' situation should be avoided. To this extent, some interviewees refers to the overreliance on theoretical frameworks and modeling languages and call for a pragmatic EA approach. Another group of interviewees highlights the need for architects to be involved with current (short-term) business needs and projects.

Furthermore, the need for keeping track of architectural decisions is brought forward by multiple experts. One interviewee claims that not documenting architectural decisions leads to the creation of architectural debt. Nevertheless, most experts claim to refrain from documenting architectural decisions. This indicates that keeping track of those decisions remains a challenge in practice. Furthermore, while there is research on supporting design rationale via UML, there is a lack of good tools in practice [43]. For example, ArchiMate does not (yet) support the documentation of design rationale [51]. Since ArchiMate is continuously updated by practitioners, it is expected that if there is a need to document these decisions using ArchiMate, this would exist [34, 50]. This contradicts the interviewees, who state that this is desirable. It might be the case that practitioners have other priorities in practice. Indeed, in many organizations, there is still a lack of documentation on EA, let alone documentation of design rationale.

Next, some experts state that the heterogeneous landscape of modeling languages complicates traceability as these languages all take a different abstraction of reality. Other experts say that the heterogeneous landscape is not a challenge regarding traceability. This second group of experts refers to the principle of the doorkeeper to provide traceability through communication at the point between two levels of abstraction. However, providing traceability via communication is questionable. Nevertheless, they do confirm the research of Verelst et al. in that there exist Functional/Constructive gaps between the different layers [52].

In addition, regarding providing and maintaining traceability, most interviewees refer to a cost-benefit tradeoff. This statement is strengthened by one insight in particular: even in a mature organization in terms of EA, IT governance, and traceability, a tradeoff is made. More specifically, this organization uses the tool MEGA at the level of IT architecture to model all AS-IS and TO-BE states. However, on the level of business architecture, only an overview of the capabilities per department is available. This lack of an AS-IS architecture on the business architecture level, given that the organization is mature in terms of EA, raises questions about the maintainability of the business architecture and the traceability to more technical architectural states.

Furthermore, one interviewee stated that the effort needed to keep models up to date and maintain traceability increases with the amount of detail included in the models. These details increase the probability of CEs, which would negatively impact the maintainability of the models [45, 48]. Moreover, one expert, who swears by a pragmatic approach using Excel and PowerPoint, argued that it is relatively easy to keep his models up-to-date. However, the amount of detail included in his models was limited (e.g., data flowing between applications, and business services were, among others, not included). In contrast, multiple experts that relied on more advanced modeling languages and tools for EA modeling, like ArchiMate, argued that the question always is 'how far you want to go ?' because each level of detail requires more effort. This may be an indication that CEs hinder traceability depending on the level of detail in EA models.

In conclusion, while practitioners and researchers claim that EA strengthens alignment between business and IT, the interview results show that there is in fact a huge lack of traceability within this domain. Thus, it is possible to speak of an 'EA & traceability paradox'.

4.3 Software Development

First of all, some interviewees claim that direct traceability from architecture to the code is not desirable since there is a timing difference between architecture and software development. In addition, multiple experts point out that traceability from architecture to code is unrealistic because code changes continuously. Nevertheless, other interviewees state that keeping EA models up to date is a big challenge without traceability to the code. Moreover, it is also argued that traceability between architecture and code is unrealistic, considering the multiple architectural versions that typically exist within organizations (i.e., various TO-BE versions that change over time). To conclude, there is a lot of disagreement on the realizability and value of traceability to code.

Second, multiple interviewees refer to the existence of ripple effects in software. Moreover, they argue that those ripple effects hinder impact analysis and traceability. This is closely related to the research on CEs by Mannaert et al. [45, 47]. In addition, one interviewee claims that software is rarely of high quality because top-notch programmers are difficult to attract, and the domain of software has become increasingly complex. He argues that such lower-quality software leads to problems like ripple effects and technical debt. Hereby, the expert confirms research on CEs that highlights the lack of a consistent application of software principles by human programmers [45].

Thirdly, some experts argue that requirements traceability is not realizable because of the size of technical requirements. Nevertheless, there is extensive research on providing requirements traceability [41, 42]. Moreover, one interviewee claims that there is a lack of tools to link requirements to architecture. However, for example, ArchiMate contains aggregation relationships to trace requirements and ways to group requirements [42]. Nonetheless, as with all traceability domains and issues, maintainability is a challenge. One expert claims that the lack of requirements traceability leads to issues such as obsolete requirements that have not been removed. This leads to unclarity on the eventual requirements that need to be or have been implemented.

Next, most experts argue that it is unrealistic to provide traceability on the flow from business to IT by using the same language. In the literature, support for this statement can be found. Research focuses on linking languages rather than creating one universal language [31, 39, 40]. However, on the level of software development, using the same language in models and code has been brought forward to provide traceability [53].

Finally, most experts point out that maintaining traceability and models over time requires considerable manual effort. Consequentially, it is often a question of costs and benefits. Therefore, some interviewees state that traceability links should be automatically maintained. Nevertheless, documentation and traceability links should, first of all, be developed. The interviews clarified that most organizations still need help with that first step. Thus, while academic experts and practitioners agree that there is value in automatically maintaining traceability, most organizations' priority is to create a mature modeling and documentation approach on the entire flow from business to IT.

4.4 Interview Results Per Interviewee (Type)

To give some insight into the distribution of the interview results, especially of the differences between groups of interviewees, Table 3 provides an overview of some important interview results per interviewee type, namely the less and the more mature organization in terms of EA, and the experts (hereafter, respectively type A, B, and C).

Table 3. Interview results grouped per type of interviewee/case

A	The importance of traceability is denied or neglected and support for EA at the top is negligeable. Moreover, EA is positioned under IT and architects are not involved in strategic decision making Claim that there is an overreliance on theoretical frameworks and modeling languages and call for a pragmatic EA approach. Moreover, traceability maintenance is not on the agenda
B	The importance of traceability is recognized in some cases, often depending on the traceability domain or issue. There is an EA culture and a division between business & IT architects Architects are involved with current business needs. In terms of traceability maintenance, the organizations refers to a cost/benefit trade-off
C	The importance of traceability is recognized, but there are often other priorities in practice. Moreover, support for EA is present, but EA positioned under IT and is (almost) never considered at the strategy level Traceability maintenance is often considered impossible or a too big investment The lack of requirements traceability in practice often leads to incorrect and inaccurate documentation and implementation of requirements

4.5 The Multidimensionality of Traceability in IT

The research results shows that traceability is indeed important in the domains of IT governance, EA, and software development. Unfortunately, these domains and their respective traceability issues are considered and treated separately in both theory and practice. This is surprising as these domains are interrelated during project delivery. Therefore, the three traceability domains should be integrated to business to code traceability. In other words, there is a need for multidimensional views on traceability in IT. Research should focus on multidimensional traceability questions, such as "Could governance frameworks like COBIT align with ArchiMate traceability mechanisms?" or "Could ArchiMate be better aligned to code?". Such research should not be limited to theory, but should also include empirical validation on realistic software systems.

5   Conclusions and Discussion

Traceability is a central concept in the domain of Enterprise Engineering, providing the crucial link between layers or steps in systems development, ranging from strategy to production code. In this age of increasing agility, traceability is a key driver in reacting to change. This paper's main contribution is twofold. First of all, traceability has seldomly been defined in such a broad and holistic manner in scientific literature. Secondly, there is little detailed empirical research on traceability in academic literature.

This research indicates that opinions on the value and importance of traceability vary greatly, along with the views on how realistic it is to establish traceability in practice. In several cases, there is little explicit attention for the concept, and tool support is limited to productivity tools such as Excel and PowerPoint, whereas more advanced tools are available. Also ex-post evaluation of projects to their business goals are not systematically done. Several cases consider traceability a cost/benefit-issue, and therefore in a sense, optional. Even in a mature EA organization, traceability remains difficult to realize.

This is remarkable in general, given the importance of traceability, but more specifically because available theories and frameworks do not seem to be applied in many cases, even though they are not completely unknown to the interviewees. For example, in the context of EA, several interviewees refrain from the use of EA frameworks or languages, even though ArchiMate for example does provide certain features in terms of traceability. Also, EA design decisions are not always documented, which is a prerequisite for traceability. Furthermore, we pointed out that this leads to a paradoxical situation: while practitioners and researchers claim that EA strengthens alignment between business and IT, the interview results show that there is in fact a huge lack of traceability within this domain in practice. In the context of IT governance, alignment is a central concept, which is intrinsically linked to traceability in the upper layers of the business-IT spectrum. However, most interviewees agree that traceability between the (business) strategy and the architecture is a challenge, even taking into account standards such as COBIT, which aims to increase alignment in practice and therefore also traceability.

Clearly, there is a gap between theory and practice regarding traceability. The reasons for this are not entirely clear from this research. One reason could be that the fragmented landscape of available theories and frameworks lack sufficiently concrete guidance and tools for practitioners to use them in the stringent environments of highly complex, time- and budget-based projects. The result is that practitioners have highly varying insights and approaches to the traceability, with traceability levels probably varying widely across teams, projects and organizations. This fragmented landscape also likely features specialized teams of architects, developers and business managers, each having their own knowledge bases. While this specialization has obvious advantages, we remark that specialization does imply integration and traceability issues which are cross-team instead of intra-team, which increases communication and traceability challenges.

These traceability challenges are far from ideal given the current trend to agile companies, where reactions to business changes require accurate and fast impact analyses, which depend on some form of traceability. Possibly, recent breakthroughs in code generation such as low code systems may contribute to this issue, as the automated production of code reduces the variation in code bases across teams and projects. However, at the upper layers in the business-IT spectrum, other initiatives are required to link governance, enterprise architectures and software development layers together. We therefore call for multi-dimensional views on traceability, providing new theoretical and practical insights into traceability especially across these three domains, its feasibility and value, tools and concrete guidelines to support practitioners aiming to deliver future-ready projects including advanced and documented traceability instruments. Enterprise Engineering as a research domain focusing on applying engineering principles and methodologies to enterprises, would be very well suited to foster this type of research.

References

1. Ahlemann, F., Stettiner, E., Messerschmidt, M., Legner, C.: Strategic Enterprise Architecture Management: Challenges, Best Practices, and Future Developments. Springer, Heidelberg (2012)
2. Samambumrthy, V., Bharadwaj, A., Grover, V.: Shaping agility through digital options: reconceptualizing the role of information technology in contemporary firms. MIS Q. **27**(2), 237–263 (2003). https://doi.org/10.2307/30036530
3. Mckinsey website, Is the Solow Paradox back. https://www.mckinsey.com/capabilities/mckinsey-digital/our-insights/is-the-solowparadox-back. Accessed 27 Aug 2023
4. The Nobel Foundation, website, Robert M. Solow Facts. https://www.nobelprize.org/prizes/economic-sciences/1987/solow/facts/. Accessed 27 Aug 2023
5. Santos, B.D., Sussman, L.: Improving the return on IT investment: the productivity paradox. Int. J. Inf. Manage. **20**(6), 429–440 (2000). https://doi.org/10.1016/S0268-4012%2800%290 0037-2
6. Stratopoulos, T., Dehning, B.: Does successful investment in information technology solve the productivity paradox? Inf. Manag. **38**(2), 103–117 (2000). https://doi.org/10.1016/S0378-7206%2800%2900058-6
7. De Haes, S., Van Grembergen, W., Joshi, A., Huygh, T.: Enterprise Governance of Information Technology: Achieving Alignment and Value in Organizations. 3rd edn. Springer Nature, Switzerland (2020)
8. Middleton, P., Harper, K.: Organizational alignment: a precondition for information systems success? J. Chang. Manag.Manag. **4**(4), 327–338 (2004). https://doi.org/10.1080/146970104 2000303820
9. Van Nuffel, D., Huysmans, P., Bellens, D., Ven, K.: Towards deterministically constructing organizations based on the normalized systems approach. In: Winter, R., Zhao, J.L., Aier, S. (eds.) Global Perspectives on Design Science Research. DESRIST 2010, LNCS, vol. 6105, pp. 242–257. Springer, Berlin (2010). https://doi.org/10.1007/978-3-642-13335-0_17
10. Klein, H.K., Myers, M.D.: A set of principles for conducting and evaluating interpretive field studies in information systems. MIS Q. **23**(1), 67–94 (1999). https://doi.org/10.2307/249410
11. Benbasat, I., Goldstein, D.K., Mead, M.: The case research strategy in studies of information systems. MIS Q. **11**(3), 369–386 (1987). https://doi.org/10.2307/248684
12. Myers, M. D.: Qualitative Research in Business and Management. 3rd editions. SAGE Publications Ltd, Thousand Oaks (2019)
13. Yin, R.K.: Case study research: design and methods. SAGE J. **19**(3), 321–332 (2013). https://doi.org/10.1177/1356389013497081
14. Beverland, M., Lindgreen, A.: What makes a good case study? A positivist review of qualitative case research. Ind. Mark. Manage. **39**(1), 56–63 (2010). https://doi.org/10.1177/135638 9013497081
15. Runseson, P., Höst, M.: Guidelines for conducting and reporting case study research in software engineering. Empir. Softw. Eng.. Softw. Eng. **14**(2), 131–164 (2009). https://doi.org/10. 1007/s10664-008-9102-8
16. Morse, J.M.: Critical analysis of strategies for determining rigor in qualitative inquiry. Qual. Health Res. **25**(9), 1212–1222 (2015). https://doi.org/10.1177/1049732315588501

17. Eisenhardt, K.M.: Building theories from case study research. Acad. Manag. Rev.Manag. Rev. **14**(4), 532–550 (1989). https://doi.org/10.5465/amr.1989.4308385
18. Göran, G.: The generation of qualitative data in information systems research: the diversity of empirical research methods. Commun. Assoc. Inf. Syst. 572–599 (2019). https://doi.org/10.17705/1CAIS.04428
19. ISO/IEC/IEEE international standard: systems and software engineering: vocabulary. In: IEEE, p. 536 (2017)
20. Mäder, P., Gotel, O.: Towards automated traceability maintenance. J. Syst. Softw.Softw. **85**(10), 2205–2227 (2012). https://doi.org/10.1016/j.jss.2011.10.023
21. Souali, K., Rahmaoui, O., Ouzzif, M.: An overview of traceability: definitions and techniques. In: 4th IEEE International Colloquium on Information Science and Technology (CiSt), pp. 789–793. IEEE, Tangier, Morocco (2016)
22. De Haes, S., van Grembergen, W., Joshi, A., Hugh, T.: Enterprise Governance of Information Technology: Achieving Alignment and Value in Organizations. 2 edn. Springer, Switzerland (2020)
23. Weill, P.D., Ross, J.W.: IT Governance: How Top Performers Manage IT Decision Rights for Superior Results. Harvard Business School Press, Boston, Massachusetts
24. Simonsson, M., Johnson, P., Ekstedt, M.: The effect of IT governance maturity on IT governance performance. Inf. Syst. Manage. **27**(1), 10–24 (2010). https://doi.org/10.1080/10580530903455106
25. Wu, S. P.-J., Straub, D. W., Liang, T.-P.: How information technology governance mechanisms and strategic alignment influence organizations performance: insights from a matched survey of business and IT managers. MIS Q. **39**, 497–518 (2015). https://doi.org/10.25300/MISQ%2F2015%2F39.2.10
26. ISACA: COBIT 2019 Framework: Governance and Management Objectives
27. Amdahl, F.S., Blaauw, G.A., Brooks, F.P.: Architecture of the IBM system/360. IBM J. Res. Dev. **44**, 21–36 (1964). https://doi.org/10.1147/rd.441.0021
28. Dijkstra, E.W.: Notes on structured programming. 2nd edn. Technisch Hogeschool Eindhoven, Eindhoven (1970)
29. Op 't Land, M., Proper, E., Waage, M., Cloo, J., Steghuis, C.: Enterprise Architecture – Creating Value by Informed Governance. Springer, Heidelberg (2009). https://doi.org/10.1007/978-3-540-85232-2
30. Jonkers, H.M., Lankhorst, M.M., Buuren, R.V., Hoppenbrouwers, S., Bonsangue, M.M., van der Torre, L.: Concepts for modeling enterprise architectures. Int. J. Cooperative Inf. Syst. **13**, 257-287 (2004). https://doi.org/10.1142/S0218843004000985
31. Engelsman, W., Wieringa, R.J., van Sinderen, M., Gordijn, J., Haaker, T.: Realizing traceability from the business model to enterprise architecture. In: Guizzardi, G., Gailly, F., Suzana Pitangueira Maciel, R. (eds.) Advances in Conceptual Modeling, ER 2019, LNCS, vol. 11787, pp. 37–46. Springer, Cham (2019). https://doi.org/10.1007/978-3-030-34146-6_4
32. The Open Group: The TOGAF Standard - 10th edition. (2022)
33. Zachman, J.A.: A framework for information systems architecture. IBM Syst. J. **38**, 454–470 (1987). https://doi.org/10.1147/sj.382.0454
34. The open group: ArchiMate 3.1 specification (2019)
35. Gerber, A., Kotzé, P., Merwe, A.V.D.: Towards the formalisation of the TOGAF content metamodel using ontologies. In: 12th International Conference on Enterprise Information Systems, ICEIS, vol. 5, pp. 54–65, Funchal, Madeira, Portugal (2010). https://doi.org/10.5220/0002903200540064
36. Antoniol, G. Canfora, G., Casazza, G., Lucia, A.D., Merlo, E.: Recovering traceability links between code and documentation. IEEE Trans. Softw. Eng. **28**, 970-983 (2002). https://doi.org/10.1109/TSE.2002.1041053

37. Murta, L.G.P., van der Hoek, A., Werner, C.M.L.: Continuous and automated evolution of architecture-to-implementation traceability links. Autom. Soft. Eng. **15**, 75–107 (2008)
38. van Gils, B.: Strategy and architecture – reconciling worldviews. In: Proper, E., Harmsen, F., Dietz, J.L.G. (eds.) Advances in Enterprise Engineering II. PRET 2009. LNBIP, vol. 28, pp. 181–196. Springer, Berlin (2009). https://doi.org/10.1007/978-3-642-01859-6_10
39. Lankhorst, M.: Enterprise Architecture at Work. 4th edn. Springer, Heidelberg (2017). https://doi.org/10.1007/978-3-662-53933-0
40. Gill, A.: Agile enterprise architecture modelling: evaluating the applicability and integration of six modelling standards. Inf. Softw. Technol.Softw. Technol. **67**, 196–206 (2015). https://doi.org/10.1016/J.INFSOF.2015.07.002
41. Plataniotis, G., Ma, Q., Proper, E. de Kinderen, S.: Traceability and modeling requirements in enterprise architecture from a design rationale perspective. In: 9th International Conference on Research Challenges in Information Science (RCIS), pp. 518–519. IEEE, Athens, Greece (2015). https://doi.org/10.1109/RCIS.2015.7128916
42. Ramesh, B., Jarke, M.: Towards reference models for requirements traceability. IEEE Trans. Software Eng. **27**(1), 58–93 (2001). https://doi.org/10.1109/32.895989
43. Tang, A., Jin, Y., Han, J.: A rationale-based architecture model for design traceability and reasoning. J. Syst. Softw.Softw. **80**, 918–934 (2007). https://doi.org/10.1016/j.jss.2006.08.040
44. Wang, X., Zhou, X., Jiang, L.: A method of business and IT alignment based on Enterprise Architecture. In: International Conference on Service Operations and Logistics, and Informatics, pp. 740–745. IEEE, Beijing, China (2008). https://doi.org/10.1109/SOLI.2008.4686496
45. Mannaert, H., Verelst, J., Bruyn, P.D.: Normalized Systems Theory. Koppa, Hasselt (2016)
46. Lehman, M.M.: On understanding laws, evolution, and conservation in the large-program life cycle. J. Syst. Softw.Softw. **1**, 213–221 (1984). https://doi.org/10.1016/0164-1212%2879%2990022-0
47. Mannaert, H., Verelst, J., Ven, K.: Towards evolvable software architectures based on systems theoretic stability. Softw. Pract. Exp. **42**(1), 89–116 (2012). https://doi.org/10.1002/spe.1051
48. Van Nuffel, D., Huysmans, P., Bellens, D., Ven, K.: Towards deterministically constructing organizations based on the normalized systems approach. In: Winter, R., Zhao, J.L., Aier, S. (eds.) Global Perspectives on Design Science Research, DESRIST, Lecture Notes in Computer Science, vol 6105, pp. 242–257. Springer, Berlin (2010). https://doi.org/10.1007/978-3-642-13335-0_17
49. Galvao, I., Goknil, A.: Survey of traceability approaches in model-driven engineering. In: 11th IEEE International Enterprise Distributed Object Computing Conference, EDOC, p. 313. IEEE, Annapolis, MD, USA (2007). https://doi.org/10.1109/EDOC.2007.42
50. van Gils, B.: Interview on traceability/Interviewer: Anna De Vos. 04/04/2023
51. Van Gils, B. Proper, H.A.: Enterprise modelling in the age of digital transformation. In: Buchmann, R., Karagiannis, D., Kirikova, M. (eds.) The practice of Enterprise Modeling. PoEM 2018. LNBIP, vol. 335. Springer, Cham (2018). https://doi.org/10.1007/978-3-030-02302-7_16
52. Verelst, J., Silva, A.R., Mannaert, H., Ferreira, D.A., Huysmans, P.: Identifying combinatorial effects in requirements engineering. In: Proper, H.A., Aveiro, D., Gaaloul, K. (eds.) Advances in Enterprise Engineering VII, EEWC, Lecture Notes in Business Information Processing, vol. 146, pp. 88–102. Springer, Berlin (2013). https://doi.org/10.1007/978-3-642-38117-1_7
53. Le, D.M., Dang, D.-H., Nguyen, V.-H.: On domain driven design using annotation-based domain specific language. Comput. Lang. Syst. Struct.. Lang. Syst. Struct. **54**, 199–235 (2018). https://doi.org/10.1016/j.cl.2018.05.001

Author Index

M. Malinova Mandelburger et al. (Eds.): EDEWC 2023, LNBIP 510, p. 123, 2024.
https://doi.org/10.1007/978-3-031-58935-5

Printed in the United States
by Baker & Taylor Publisher Services